edexcel
advancing learning, changing lives

BTEC First
Business

STUDY GUIDE

D0315763

A PEARSON COMPANY

BTEC First Study Guide: Business

Published by:
Edexcel Limited
One90 High Holborn
London WC1V 7BH
www.edexcel.org.uk

Distributed by:
Pearson Education Limited
Edinburgh Gate
Harlow
Essex CM20 2JE

First published 2007

Seventh impression 2009

ISBN 978-1-84690-169-0

Project managed, designed and typeset by Bookcraft Ltd, Stroud, Gloucestershire
Printed by Ashford Colour Press Ltd, Gosport

Cover image © JLImages/Alamy

The Publisher's policy is to use paper manufactured from sustainable forests.

All reasonable efforts have been made to trace and contact original copyright owners.

Contents

Preface

Following a BTEC programme is an exciting way to study. It gives you the opportunity to develop the knowledge, skills and understanding that you will need in the world of work.

BTECs are very different from GCSEs; a BTEC puts *you* in charge of your own learning. This guide has been written specially for you, to help you get started and succeed on your BTEC First course.

The **introduction**, Your BTEC First, tells you about your new course. This will be your companion through the BTEC First, as it:

- tells you how your BTEC will differ from GCSE;

- suggests how you can plan your time;

- explains ways to make the most of visits, guest speakers and work experience;

- advises you about resources and how to find information;

- gives you advice on making presentations and doing assignments.

The **activities** give you tasks to do on your own, in small groups or as a class. You will have the opportunity to put into practice the theory you learn. The activities will help you prepare for assessment by practising your skills and showing you how much you know. These activities are *not* intended for assessment.

The sample **marked assignments** (also sometimes called marked assessments) show you what other students have done to gain a Pass, Merit or Distinction. By seeing what past students have done, you should be able to improve your own grade.

Your BTEC First will cover either three or six units, depending on whether you are doing a Certificate or a Diploma. In this guide the activities cover Unit 1 'Exploring Business Purposes'. This sets the scene for your study of business, and also links in to many of the other units you may study.

Because the guide covers only one unit, it is important that you do all the other work your tutor sets you. Your tutor will ask you to research information in textbooks, in the library and on the internet. You may also have your own textbook for the course: use it! You should have the chance to visit local organisations or welcome guest speakers to your institution. This is a great way to find out more about your chosen vocational area – the type of jobs that are available and what the work is really like.

This guide is a taster, an introduction to your BTEC First. Use it as such, and make the most of the rich learning environment that your tutors will provide for you. Your BTEC First will give you an excellent base for further study, a broad understanding of business and the knowledge you need to succeed in the world of work.

Your BTEC First

Starting a new course is often both exciting and scary. It's normally exciting to do something new, and this includes learning different subjects that appeal to you. BTEC First courses are work-related, so you will be focusing on the work area that interests you. It can be nerve-wracking, though, if you are worried that there may be some topics that you will not understand, if you are unsure how you will be assessed, or if the prospect of some aspects of the course – such as finding out information on your own, or giving a presentation – makes your blood run cold!

It may help to know that these are worries are common to many new BTEC First students. Yet every year thousands of them thoroughly enjoy their courses and successfully achieve the award.

Some do this the easy way, while others find it harder.

The easy way involves two things:

- knowing about the course and what you have to do

- positive thinking

Knowledge of the course means that you focus your time and energy on the things that matter. Positive thinking means that you aren't defeated before you start. Your ability to do well is affected by what goes on in your mind. A positive attitude helps you to meet new challenges more easily.

This guide has been written to give you all the information you need to get the most out of your course, to help you to develop positive thinking skills, and, of course, to help you successfully achieve your award. Keep it nearby throughout your course and re-read the relevant parts whenever you need to.

DO THINK	DON'T THINK
I'm quite capable of doing well on this course. First I need to check what I know about it and what I don't – and to fill in the gaps.	*If I struggle a bit or don't like something then so what? I can always drop out if I can't cope.*

Knowing about your course

If a friend or relative asked about your course, what would you say? Would you just shrug or give a vague comment? Or could you give a short, accurate description? If you can do this it usually means that you have a better understanding of what your course is all about – which means you are likely to be better prepared and better organised. You are also more likely to make links between your course and the world around you. This means you can be alert to information that relates to the subject you are studying.

→   Your family, friends, or other people you know may talk about topics that you are covering in class.

→   There may be programmes on television which relate to your studies.

→   Items in the news may be relevant.

→   You may work in a part-time job. Even if your part-time work is in a different area, there will still be useful links. For example, for most BTEC First courses you need to know how to relate to other people at work, how to assist your customers or clients and how to communicate properly. These are skills you need in most part-time jobs.

If you have only a hazy idea about your course then it is sensible to re-read any information you have been given by your school or college and to check further details on the Edexcel website at www.edexcel.org.uk. At the very least, you should know:

•   the type of BTEC award you are aiming for and how many units you will be taking:

◊   BTEC First Diploma – normally taken as a full-time course, with six units

◊   BTEC First Certificate – may be taken as a full-time or part-time course, with three units

•   the titles of your core units and what they cover

•   the number of specialist units you must take and the options available to you

Core units are compulsory for all students at all centres, and you can find details of them on the Edexcel website. The range of specialist units you can choose will depend upon which award you are taking and where you are studying. Many centres design their courses to meet the needs of the students in their area, in which case you won't have complete freedom to choose your own options. If you do have a choice, find out the content of each of the specialist units available, then think carefully about the ones you would most like to study. Then talk through your ideas with your tutor before you make a final decision.

DO THINK	DON'T THINK
The more I know about my course, the more I can link the different parts together and see how they relate to other areas of my life. This will give me a better understanding of the subjects I am studying.	*It's unlikely that any course will have much relevance to my life or my interests, no matter what anyone says.*

Knowing the difference: BTEC First versus GCSE

BTEC First awards are different from GCSEs in several ways. In addition to the differences in content, the way the topics are taught and the tutors' expectations of their students are also often different. Knowing about these gives you a better idea of what to expect – and how you should respond.

→ BTEC First awards are work-related. All the topics you learn relate to the skills and knowledge you will need in the workplace.

→ They are practical. You will learn how to apply your knowledge, both on your own and as a member of a team, to develop your skills and abilities.

→ Most full-time BTEC First Diploma courses in colleges are completed in one year. If you are taking a BTEC First Certificate course alongside your GCSEs, then you will probably be doing this over two years.

→ There are no exams. So you won't be expected to revise and learn lots of facts, or to write answers to questions in a hot exam room next June. Instead, you will complete assignments set by your tutors, based on learning outcomes set by Edexcel. You can read more about assignments on page 19, but for now you can think of them as being similar to coursework. They will be given to you through the year, and each will have a deadline. See page 19 for advice on coping with assignments, and page 9 for advice on managing your time effectively.

→ On a BTEC First course you will achieve Pass, Merit and Distinctions in your assignments. You will then be awarded an overall Pass, Merit or Distinction for the whole course.

→ BTEC First students are encouraged to take responsibility for their own learning. Your tutors won't expect to have to stand over you all the time to check what you are doing. This helps you to develop the skills to be mature and independent at work. You will be expected to be keen and interested enough to work hard without being continually monitored. You will also be expected to become more self-reliant and better organised as the course progresses. Some students thrive in this situation. They love having more freedom, and are keen to show that they can handle it, especially when they know that they can still ask for help or support when they need it. Other students – thankfully, a minority – aren't mature enough to cope in this situation, so it goes to their head and they run wild.

→ If you've just left school and are going to study for your BTEC First in a college, then you will find many other differences. No bells or uniforms! Maybe fewer timetabled hours; probably longer lesson periods. You will mix with a wider range of people, of different ages and nationalities. You are starting a whole new phase of your life, when you will meet new people and have new experiences. However strange it may seem at the beginning, new students normally settle down quickly. Even if they have been disappointed with some of their grades at GCSE, they are relieved that they can put this disappointment behind them and have a fresh start. If this applies to you, then it's up to you to make the most of it.

DO THINK	DON'T THINK
On my BTEC First course I can find out more about the area of work that interests me. I will enjoy proving that I can work just as well with less direct supervision, and know I can get help and support when I need it.	*Doing a BTEC First will be great because the tutors won't be breathing down my neck all the time and won't care if I mess around on the course.*

Knowing how to use your time

How well organised are you? Do you always plan in advance, find what you've put away, and remember what you've promised to do without being reminded? Or do you live for the moment – and never know what you will be doing more than six hours in advance? Would you forget who you were, some days, unless someone reminded you?

School teachers cope with young students like this by giving homework on set nights, setting close deadlines, and regularly reminding everyone when work is due. They don't (or daren't!) ask students to do something over the next couple of months and then just leave them to it.

Although your BTEC First tutor will give you reminders, he or she will also be preparing you for higher-level courses and for having a responsible job – when you will be expected to cope with a range of tasks and deadlines with few, if any, reminders. On your BTEC First course some work will need to be completed quickly and done for the next session. But other tasks may take some time to do – such as finding out information on a topic, or preparing a presentation. You may be set tasks like this several weeks in advance of the deadline, and it can be easy to put them off, or to forget them altogether – with the result that you may not do the task at all, or end up doing a sloppy job at the last minute because you haven't had time to do it properly.

This problem gets worse over time. At the start of a new course there always seems to be a lot of time and not much pressure: the major deadlines may seem far in the future, and you may find it easy to cope day by day.

This situation is unlikely to last. Some tasks may take you longer than you had thought. Several tutors may want work completed at the same time. And deadlines have a nasty habit of speeding up as they approach. If you have lots of personal commitments too, then you may struggle to cope, and get very stressed or be tempted to give up.

The best way to cope is to learn to manage your own time, rather than letting it manage you. The following tips may help.

→ Expect to have work to do at home, both during the week and at weekends, and plan time for this around your other commitments. It's unrealistic to think that you can complete the course without doing much at home.

→ Schedule fixed working times into your week, taking your other commitments into account. For example, if you always play five-a-side football on Monday evening, keep Tuesday evening free for catching up with work. Similarly, if you work every Saturday, keep some time free on Sunday for work you have to complete over the weekend.

→ Get into the habit of working at certain times, and tell other people in your life what you are doing. If you've no work to do on one of these days, then that's a bonus. It's always easier to find something to do when you unexpectedly have free time than to find time for a task you didn't expect.

→ Write down exactly what you have to do in a diary or notebook the moment you are told about it, so that you don't waste time doing the wrong thing – or ringing lots of people to find out if they know what it is you're supposed to be doing.

→ Normally you should do tasks in order of urgency – even if this means you can't start with the one you like the best. But if, for example, you need to send off for information and wait for it to arrive, you can use the time to work on less urgent tasks.

→ Don't forget to include in your schedule tasks that have to be done over a period of time. It's easy to forget these if you have lots of shorter deadlines to meet. Decide how long the whole task is likely to take you, break the total time up into manageable chunks, and allocate enough time to complete it by the deadline date.

→ Always allow more time than you think you will need, never less.

→ Be disciplined! Anyone who wants to get on in life has to learn that there are times when you have to work, even if you don't want to. Try rewarding yourself with a treat afterwards.

→ If you are struggling to motivate yourself, set yourself a shorter time limit and really focus on what you are doing to get the most out of the session. You may be so engrossed when the time is up that you want to carry on.

→ Speak to your tutor promptly if you have a clash of commitments or a personal problem that is causing you serious difficulties – or if you have truly forgotten an important deadline (then vow not to do so again)!

→ If few of these comments apply to you because you are well organised, hard-working and regularly burn the midnight oil trying to get everything right, then don't forget to build leisure time and relaxation into your schedule. And talk to your tutor if you find that you are getting stressed out because you are trying too hard to be perfect.

DO THINK	DON'T THINK
I am quite capable of planning and scheduling the work I have to do, and being self-disciplined about doing it. I don't need a tutor to do this for me.	*I can only work when I'm in the mood and it's up to my tutors to remind me what to do and when.*

Knowing about resources

Resources for your course include the handouts you are given by your tutor, the equipment and facilities at your school or college (such as the library and resource centre), and information you can obtain on the internet from websites that relate to your studies. Resources that are essential for your course – such as a computer and access to the internet – will always be provided. The same applies to specialist resources required for a particular subject. Other resources – such as paper, file folders and a pen – you will be expected to provide yourself.

→ Some popular (or expensive) resources may be shared, and may need to be reserved in advance. These may include popular textbooks in the library, and laptop computers for home use. If it's important to reserve this resource for a certain time, don't leave it till the last minute.

→ You can only benefit from a resource if you know how to use it properly. This applies, for example, to finding information in the library, or using PowerPoint to prepare a presentation. Always ask for help if you need it.

→ You cannot expect to work well if you are forever borrowing what you need. Check out the stationery and equipment you need to buy yourself, and do so before the course starts. Many stationers have discounts on stationery near the start of term.

→ Look after your resources, to avoid last-minute panics or crises. For example, file handouts promptly and in the right place, follow the guidelines for using your IT system, and replace items that are lost or have ceased to work.

DO THINK	DON'T THINK
I have all the resources I need for my course, and I know how to use them or how to find out.	*I can find out what's available if and when I need it, and I can always cadge stuff from someone else.*

Knowing how to get the most from work experience

On some BTEC First courses – such as Children's Care, Learning and Development – all students must undertake a related work placement. On others, work placements are recommended but not essential, or may be required only for some specialist units. So whether or not you spend time on work experience will depend upon several factors, including the course you are taking, the units you are studying, and the opportunities in your own area. You will need to check with your tutor to find out whether you will be going on a work placement as part of your course.

If you need evidence from a work placement for a particular unit, then your tutor will give you a log book or work diary, and will help you to prepare for the experience. You should also do your best to help yourself.

Your placement

→   Check you have all the information about the placement you need, such as the address, start time, and name of your placement supervisor.

→   Know the route from home and how long it will take you to get there.

→   Know what is suitable to wear, and what is not – and make sure all aspects of your appearance are appropriate to your job role.

→   Know any rules, regulations or guidelines that you must follow.

→   Check you know what to do if you have a problem during the placement, such as being too ill to go to work.

→   Talk to your tutor if you have any special personal worries or concerns.

→ Understand why you are going on the placement and how it relates to your course.

→ Know the units to which your evidence will apply.

→ Check the assessment criteria for the units and list the information and evidence you will need to obtain.

DO THINK

Work experience gives me the opportunity to find out more about possible future workplaces, and link my course to reality.

DON'T THINK

Work experience just means I'll be given all the boring jobs to do.

Knowing how to get the most from special events

BTEC First courses usually include several practical activities and special events. These make the work more interesting and varied, and give you the opportunity to find out information and develop your skills and knowledge in new situations. They may include visits to external venues, visits from specialist speakers, and team events.

Some students enjoy the chance to do something different, while others can't see the point. It will depend on whether or not you are prepared to take an active involvement in what is happening. You will normally obtain the most benefit if you make a few preparations beforehand.

→ Listen carefully when any visit outside school or college, or any arrangement for someone to visit you, is being described. Check you understand exactly why this has been organised and how it relates to your course.

→ Find out what you are expected to do, and any rules or guidelines you must follow, including any specific requirements related to your clothes or appearance.

→ Write down all the key details, such as the date, time, location, and names of those involved. Always allow ample time so that you arrive five minutes early for any special event, and are never late.

→ Your behaviour should be impeccable whenever you are on a visit or listening to a visiting speaker.

→   Check the information you will be expected to prepare or obtain. Often this will relate to a particular assignment, or help you understand a particular topic in more detail.

→   For an external visit, you may be expected to write an account of what you see or do, or to use what you learn to answer questions in an assignment. Remember to take a notebook and pen with you, so that you can make notes easily.

→   For an external speaker, you may be expected to prepare a list of questions as well as to make notes during the talk. Someone will also need to say 'thank you' afterwards on behalf of the group. If your class wants to tape the talk, it's polite to ask the speaker for permission first.

→   For a team event, you may be involved in planning and helping to allocate different team roles. You will be expected to participate positively in any discussions, to talk for some (but not all) of the time, and perhaps to volunteer for some jobs yourself.

→   Write up any notes you make during the event neatly as soon as possible afterwards – while you can still understand what you wrote!

DO THINK	DON'T THINK
I will get more out of external visits, visiting speakers and team events if I prepare in advance, and this will also help me to get good grades.	*Trips out and other events are just a good excuse to have a break and take it easy for bit.*

Knowing how to find out information

Many students who are asked to find out information find it difficult to do so effectively. If they are online, they often print out too much, or can't find what they want. Similarly, too many students drift aimlessly around a library rather than purposefully search for what they need.

Finding out information is a skill that you need to learn. You need to know where to look, how to recognise appropriate information, and when to stop looking in order to meet your deadline, as well as what to do with the information when you've found it.

The first thing to realise is that you will never be asked to find out information for no reason. Before you start, you need to know what you are looking for, why it is needed, where you can find it, and the deadline.

This means you target your search properly and start looking in the right place.

Researching in the library

→   Find out the order in which books are stored. This is normally explained to all students during their induction.

→   Know the other resources and facilities that are available in your library besides books – for example, CD-ROMs and journals.

→   Take enough change with you so that you can photocopy articles that you can't remove. Remember to write down the source of any article you photocopy.

→   If you need specific books or articles, and aren't sure where they will be, try to visit during a quiet time, when the librarian can give you help if you need it.

→   If you find two or three books which include the information you need, that's normally enough. Too many can be confusing.

→   Check quickly if a book contains the information you need by looking in the index for the key words and then checking you can understand the text. If you can't, then forget it and choose another. A book is only helpful to you if you can follow it.

Researching online

→   Use a good search engine to find relevant websites. Scroll down the first few pages of the search results and read the descriptions to see which sites seem to be the best.

→   Remember to read all parts of the screen to check what's available on a website, as menus may be at the foot of the page as well as at the top or on either side. Many large sites have a search facility or a site map which you can access if you are stuck.

→   Don't get distracted by irrelevant information. If your searches regularly lead nowhere, ask your IT resource staff for help.

→   Don't print out everything you read. Even if printouts are free, too much information is just confusing.

→   Bookmark sites you use regularly and find helpful.

Researching by asking other people

This doesn't mean asking someone else to do the work for you! It means finding out about a topic by asking an expert.

→ Think about the people you know who might be able to help you because they have knowledge or experience that would be useful.

→ Prepare in advance by thinking about the best questions to ask.

→ Then contact the person and (unless you know the person well) introduce yourself.

→ Explain politely and clearly why you need the information.

→ Ask your questions, but don't gabble or ask them too quickly.

→ Write notes, so that you don't forget what you are told. Put the name and title of the person, and the date, at the top of the first page.

→ Ask if you can contact the person again, in case there is anything you need to check. Write down their phone number or email address.

→ Remember to say 'thank you'.

Using your information

→ Keep all your information on a topic neatly in a labelled folder or file. If you think you might want to reuse the folder later, put the title on in pencil rather than ink.

→ Refresh your memory of the task by re-reading it before you start to sift the information. Then only select pages that are relevant to the question you have been asked. Put all the other paper away.

→ Remember that you will rarely just be asked to reproduce the information that you have obtained. You will need to make decisions about which parts are the most relevant and how you should use these. For example, if you have visited a sports facility to find out what is available, then you may have to explain which activities are targeted at certain groups of people. You would be expected to disregard information that didn't relate to that task. Or you may be asked to evaluate the facilities, in which case you would have to consider how well the centre met the needs of its users and how it could do better.

→ Never rewrite copied information and pretend they are your own words! This is plagiarism, which is a serious offence with severe penalties. You need to state the source of your material by including the name of the author or the web address – either in the text, or as part of a list at the end. Your tutor will show you how to do this if you are not sure.

→ Write a draft and then ask your tutor to confirm that you are on the right track. You can also check with your tutor if you are unsure whether or not to include certain types of information.

DO THINK	DON'T THINK
Researching can be fun, and practice makes perfect. If I'm struggling to find something or to know what to include, I'll ask for help. Then it will be easier next time.	*The more I find the better, because collecting or writing a lot always impresses people.*

Knowing how to make a presentation

Presentations are a common feature of many BTEC courses. Usually you will be asked to do a presentation as a member of a team. If the team works together and its members support each other then this is far less of an ordeal than it may first seem. The benefits are that you learn many skills, including how to be a team member, how to speak in public, and how to prepare visual aids (often using PowerPoint) – all of which are invaluable for your future career.

Many students get worried about the idea of standing up to speak in front of an audience. This is quite normal, and can even improve your performance if you know how to focus your anxieties productively!

Presentation tasks can be divided into three stages: the initial preparations, the organisation, and the delivery.

Preparation

→   Divide up the work of researching fairly among the team.

→   Bear in mind people's individual strengths and weaknesses and allow for these, so that you all gain from working as a team.

→   Work out how long each person must speak so that you don't exceed your time limit (either individually or as a team).

→   Agree on the type of visual aids that would be best, given your topic. Keeping things simple is often more effective than producing something elaborate that doesn't work properly.

→   Decide on any handouts that are required, prepare these and check them carefully.

→   Check you know when and where the presentation will be held and what you should wear.

→ Think in advance about any questions you may be asked, both individually and as a team.

Organisation

→ Decide who will start and how each person will be introduced. Sometimes the lead person introduces everyone; on other occasions people introduce themselves.

→ Decide the most logical order in which to speak, bearing in mind everyone's contribution and how it fits into the overall presentation.

→ Prepare prompt cards. It's easy to forget some of the things you want to say, so put your main points down in the right order on a prompt card. Never read from this! Instead, write clearly and neatly so that you can just glance down to check on your next point.

→ Check you have sufficient copies of any handouts, and that these are clear and easy to read.

→ Rehearse several times and check your timings.

→ Get your clothes ready the night before.

→ Arrive at the event in plenty of time so that you're not in a rush.

Delivery

→ Take a few deep breaths before you start, to calm your nerves.

→ Make eye contact with your audience, and smile.

→ Keep your head up.

→ Speak a little more slowly than usual.

→ Speak a little more loudly than usual – without shouting.

→ Answer any questions you are asked. If you don't know the answer, be honest – don't guess or waffle.

→ Offer to help a team member who is struggling to answer a question, if you know the answer.

DO THINK	DON'T THINK
If I am well prepared and organised then my presentation will be OK, even if I'm really scared. The audience will always make allowances for some nerves.	*I'm confident about speaking in public so I don't have to bother preparing in advance.*

Knowing the importance of assignments

All BTEC First students are assessed by means of assignments. Each assignment is designed to link to specific learning outcomes. Assignments let you demonstrate that you have the skills and knowledge to get a Pass, Merit or Distinction grade. At the end of your course, your assignment grades together determine the overall grade for your BTEC First Certificate or Diploma.

Each assignment you are given will comprise specific tasks. Many will involve you in obtaining information (see page 14) and then applying your new-found knowledge to produce a written piece of work. Alternatively, you may demonstrate your knowledge by giving a presentation or taking part in an activity.

To get a good grade, you must be able to produce a good response to assignments. To do so, you need to know the golden rules that apply to all assignments, then how to interpret your instructions to get the best grade you can.

The golden rules for assignments

→ Read your instructions carefully. Check that you understand everything, and ask your tutor for help if there is anything that puzzles or worries you.

→ Check that you know whether you have to do all the work on your own, or if you will have to do some as a member of a group. If you work as a team, you will always have to identify which parts are your own contribution.

→ Write down any verbal instructions you are given, including when your tutor is available to discuss your research or any drafts you have prepared.

→ Check you know the date of the final deadline and any penalties for not meeting this.

→ Make sure you know what to do if you have a serious personal problem and need an official extension. An example would be if you were ill and expected to be absent for some time.

→ Remember that copying someone else's work (plagiarism) is always a serious offence – and is easy for experienced tutors to spot. Your school or college will have strict rules which state the consequences of doing this. It is never worth the risk.

→ Schedule enough time for finding out the information and making your initial preparations – from planning a presentation to writing your first draft or preparing an activity.

→ Allow plenty of time between talking to your tutor about your plans, preparations and drafts and the final deadline.

Interpreting your instructions to get the best grade you can

→ Most assignments start with a command word – for example, 'describe', 'explain' or 'evaluate'. These words relate to the level of answer required. A higher level of response is required for a Merit grade than for a Pass, and a higher level still for a Distinction.

→ Students often fall short in an assignment because they do not realise the differences between these words and what they have to do in each case. The tables below show you what is usually required for each grade when you see a particular command word.

→ As you can see from the tables, to obtain a higher grade with a given command word (such as 'describe'), you usually need to give a more complex description or use your information in a different way. You can refer to the example answers to real assignments, and tutor comments, from page 57 onwards.

→ You can check the command words you are likely to see for each unit in the grading grid. It is sensible to read this carefully in advance, so that you know the evidence that you will have to present to obtain a Pass, Merit or Distinction grade.

→ Be prepared to amend, redraft or rethink your work following feedback from your tutor, so that you always produce work that you know is your best effort.

→ Learn how to record your achievement so that you can see your predicted overall grade. Your tutor will show you how to do this, using the Edexcel *Recording your Achievement* form for your subject.

The following tables show what is required to obtain a Pass, Merit and Distinction, for a range of different 'command words'. Generally speaking:

- To obtain a Pass grade, you must be able to show that you understand the key facts relating to a topic.

- To obtain a Merit grade, you must be able to show that, in addition to fulfilling the requirements for a Pass grade, you can also use your knowledge in a certain way.

- To obtain a Distinction grade, you must be able to show that, in addition to fulfilling the requirements for a Pass and a Merit grade, you can also apply your knowledge to a situation and give a reasoned opinion.

Obtaining a Pass

Complete...	Complete a form, diagram or drawing.
Demonstrate...	Show that you can do a particular activity.
Describe...	Give a clear, straightforward description which includes all the main points.
Identify...	Give all the basic facts which relate to a certain topic.
List...	Write a list of the main items (not sentences).
Name...	State the proper terms related to a drawing or diagram.
Outline...	Give all the main points, but without going into too much detail.
State...	Point out or list the main features.

Examples:

- *List the main features on your mobile phone.*

- *Describe the best way to greet a customer.*

- *Outline the procedures you follow to keep your computer system secure.*

Obtaining a Merit

Analyse...	Identify the factors that apply, and state how these are linked and how each of them relates to the topic.
Comment on...	Give your own opinions or views.
Compare... Contrast...	Identify the main factors relating to two or more items and point out the similarities and differences.
Competently use...	Take full account of information and feedback you have obtained to review or improve an activity.
Demonstrate...	Prove you can carry out a more complex activity.
Describe...	Give a full description including details of all the relevant features.
Explain...	Give logical reasons to support your views.
Justify...	Give reasons for the points you are making so that the reader knows what you are thinking.
Suggest...	Give your own ideas or thoughts.

Examples:

- *Explain why mobile phones are so popular.*

- *Describe the needs of four different types of customers.*

- *Suggest the type of procedures a business would need to introduce to keep its IT system secure.*

Obtaining a Distinction

Analyse...	Identify several relevant factors, show how they are linked, and explain the importance of each.
Compare... Contrast...	Identify the main factors in two or more situations, then explain the similarities and differences, and in some cases say which is best and why.
Demonstrate...	Prove that you can carry out a complex activity taking into account information you have obtained or received to adapt your original ideas.

Describe...	Give a comprehensive description which tells a story to the reader and shows that you can apply your knowledge and information correctly.
Evaluate...	Bring together all your information and make a judgement on the importance or success of something.
Explain...	Provide full details and reasons to support the arguments you are making.
Justify...	Give full reasons or evidence to support your opinion.
Recommend...	Weigh up all the evidence to come to a conclusion, with reasons, about what would be best.

Examples:

- *Evaluate the features and performance of your mobile phone.*

- *Analyse the role of customer service in contributing to an organisation's success.*

- *Justify the main features on the website of a large, successful organisation of your choice.*

DO THINK

Assignments give me the opportunity to demonstrate what I've learned. If I work steadily, take note of the feedback I get and ask for advice when I need it, there is no reason why I can't get a good grade.

DON'T THINK

If I mess up a few assignments it isn't the end of the world. All teachers like to criticise stuff, and I only wanted a Pass anyway.

Knowing what to do if you have a problem

If you are lucky, you will sail through your BTEC First with no major problems. Unfortunately, not every student is so lucky. Some may encounter personal difficulties or other issues that can seriously disrupt their work. If this happens to you, it's vitally important that you know what to do.

→   Check that you know who to talk to if you have a problem. Then check who you should see if that person happens to be away at the time.

→   Don't sit on a problem and worry about it. Talk to someone, in confidence, promptly.

→   Most schools and colleges have professional counselling staff you can see if you have a concern that you don't want to tell your tutor. They will never repeat anything you say to them without your permission.

→   If you have a serious complaint, it's a good idea to talk it over with one of your tutors before you do anything else. Schools and colleges have official procedures to cover important issues such as appeals about assignments and formal complaints, but it's usually sensible to try to resolve a problem informally first.

→   If your school or college has a serious complaint about you, it is likely to invoke its formal disciplinary procedures, and you should know what these are. If you have done something wrong or silly, remember that most people will have more respect for you if you are honest about it, admit where you went wrong and apologise promptly. Lying only makes matters worse.

→   Most students underestimate the ability of their tutors to help them in a crisis – and it's always easier to cope with a worry if you've shared it with someone.

DO THINK	DON'T THINK
My tutors are just as keen for me to do well as I am, and will do everything they can to help me if I have a problem.	*No one will believe I have a problem. Tutors just think it's an excuse to get out of working.*

Finally...

This introduction wasn't written just to give you another task to do! It was written to help you to do your best and get the most out of your course.

So don't just put it on one side and forget about it. Go back to it from time to time to remind yourself about how to approach your course. You may also find it helpful to show it to other people at home, so that they will understand more about your course and what you have to do.

Activities

1   Understanding business activities

In this section we will focus on grading criteria P1 and M1 from Unit 1 'Exploring Business Purposes'.

Activity 6 also links to grading criteria P1 and M1 from Unit 9 'Exploring Business Enterprise'.

Learning outcome

Understand the nature of business and ownership

Content

Purpose: supply of goods and services e.g. at a profit, free, at cost, for sale below cost

Ownership: e.g. sole trader; partnership; limited companies (private – Ltd, public – plc); charity; voluntary organisations; franchises; co-operatives

Size: small; small–medium; medium; large

Scale: local; regional; national; European and global organisations

Grading criteria

P1: describe four different types of business organisations in terms of purpose, ownership, size and scale

This means you will need to give details about four different business organisations and state why they are in business, how they are owned, how big they are, and the area over which they operate.

M1: compare and contrast the ownership, aims and objectives of two selected businesses

Activity 1

All businesses are in business for a purpose. They may:

- produce or sell goods
- provide services
- provide both goods and services

Task 1

Make a table like the one below. Decide on the main activity of each of the businesses listed, and put a tick in the correct column. Compare your answers with those given by other members of your class.

© Misocrazy, Flickr (Public Commons)

© Bitmapr Photos, Flickr (Public Commons)

Business	Type of activity		
	Producing or selling goods	Providing a service	Providing both goods and services
Next			
Manchester United			
Alton Towers			
Virgin Trains			
WH Smith			
PC World			
Pizza Hut			
Ikea			
Heinz			
Thomas Cook			

Task 2

In small groups, think of six businesses that you know about or use regularly, and add them to the table. Try to think of two businesses for each type of activity. Then compare your ideas with those of other groups and combine them into one table as a class.

Activity 2

Goods and services may be supplied:

- at a profit
- free of charge
- at cost price
- below cost price

Task 1

Working in small groups, make a table like the one below and tick the pricing category for each of the items. In each case, agree a reason for your choice.

In your groups, look back at the final table of businesses the class identified in Activity 1.

Identify the number of businesses that normally aim to make a profit from their goods or services. Suggest why this option is so popular.

Suggest two reasons why any of the businesses may supply their goods and services free, at cost price or for sale below cost price.

Identify three organisations in your own area that do not aim to make a profit from the goods and services they provide. Suggest the reasons for this.

Make a short presentation of your findings to the rest of the class.

Item	Pricing category				Reason
	At a profit	Free of charge	At cost price	Below cost price	
nursing care in an NHS hospital					
a prescription for medicine for a pensioner					
a prescription for an expensive medicine for your tutor					
a taxi home from hospital					
an eye test for a full-time student, under 19					
leaflets about healthy eating					
a recipe leaflet promoting products in a supermarket					
a recipe book sold in a supermarket					
unsold books being sold off by the supermarket					
last-day bargain sale to clear unsold stock					

Task 2

When the fashion store H&M launched its Stella McCartney collection in November 2005, the entire stock sold out in a day. Many of the clothes were then resold on eBay at far higher prices.

Answer these questions as a class:

- Why did the stock sell out so quickly?
- Why were many of the clothes then resellable?
- Should H&M have sold them at a higher price? Give a reason for your answer.
- If they had done so, would they have been guaranteed to make a higher profit? Give a reason for your answer.

Working individually, look at the picture on the right and decide:

- whether this business or organisation provides goods, a service or both
- why there are queues outside

Then compare your ideas as a class.

© Gerry Davies

Activity 3

Read the following descriptions of people and their businesses.

Match each person to the type of business they own (choose from A to F). Then identify the main advantages and disadvantages of each type of ownership. Use a table like this one:

Person	Type of business	Advantages	Disadvantages
		1.	1.
		2.	2.
		3.	3.

A. sole trader

B. partnership

C. private limited company

D. public limited company

E. worker cooperative

F. franchise

Louise is a hairdresser. Last year she started her own business, and she now employs an apprentice. She enjoys the fact that she is her own boss and can keep all the profits after paying tax. But she finds it difficult to keep her accounts and is aware that she is personally responsible for any debts she owes.

Joe works for a superstore. He bought shares in the company, so that he benefits if it does well. He regularly checks the share price in the newspaper and enjoys receiving a dividend twice a year. His only worry is that if the business performed poorly, the share price could drop, and the firm may be bought cheaply by a rival who may close many of the stores.

Paula and Jane started up their own mobile business last year running 'Tumble Tots' classes for young children. They feel more secure trading under an established brand name, even though this cost them an initial fee and they have to pay a percentage of their earnings. They think this is worth it for the advice and help they receive, as well as professional marketing of the business.

Waheed and Mohammed work together in their car valeting business. They rent space on a busy town-centre car park and offer to clean cars whilst their owners are shopping. They were worried at first that they may disagree or even fall out about many aspects of the business, but this hasn't happened. They know they have to consult each other about the decisions they make and are jointly and personally liable for any debts that they owe.

Andrew met his colleagues when he was at art school. They now run a design studio between them. They share the profits and make all the decisions together. Sometimes this can make decision-making slow, and occasionally people fall out – especially if some people aren't seen to be working as hard as the others.

Shahida and her brother Tariq work for the family jewellery business, started by her parents. The four own all the shares between them. They like the fact that their liability for debts is limited to the amount they each invested in the business and that all their affairs are private. No shares can be sold to members of the public. Their father owns most of the shares, so he has more votes than anyone else.

Activity 4

All the businesses described in Activity 3 are privately owned, but many people work for organisations owned by the state, and others for voluntary or not-for-profit organisations.

Task 1

Complete the table on the next page. Decide whether each of the businesses listed is privately owned, state-owned, or a voluntary or not-for-profit organisation. Compare your answers with other members of your class.

Task 2

Working in small groups, add another four organisations of each type. Then compare your ideas with those from other groups.

Task 3

Thorntons, the chocolate producer and retailer, was started by John William Thornton, who opened a sweet shop in 1911. In 1919, after his death, the business was taken over by his two sons, who formed JW Thornton Ltd in 1921. It continued to expand, and today there are over 400 shops and 160 franchises. The business was floated on the stock exchange in 1988.

Working individually, list all the different types of ownership mentioned in the paragraph about Thorntons.

Decide why each type of ownership was most appropriate for Thorntons at the time.

Activity 5

Work in small groups for this activity.

Emily is a chocolate addict and loves the idea of running a Thornton's franchise, using money she has recently inherited from her aunt. At www.thorntons.co.uk she has seen that it would cost her £12,500 for the initial franchise package and for training, help and advice. She would also have to pay for stock (between £8,000 and £25,000) and for shop fixtures and fittings (about £30,000). She would be tied into the contract for at least five years. Thorntons would deduct 2.5% from her profit margins during this time.

Alternatively, she could start her own retail business or start up a joint business with her brother and sister, Sam and Sophie, both of whom have experience in retailing and also inherited money from her aunt. Her father thinks this would be best and says it would be sensible to set up a private company. Sam disagrees and thinks they should run the firm as a partnership, whereas Sophie prefers the idea of a workers' cooperative, both for themselves and for anyone who worked for them.

Emily has come to you for advice. As a group, discuss what Emily should do. Be prepared to support your final decision with reasons. Then present your verdict to the rest of the class. Take votes at the end to see which ownership option is considered the most popular overall.

Activity 6

Task 1

As a group, decide on the experience, skills, knowledge and abilities Emily will need to be able to start her own business and run it successfully.

Task 2

Suggest how her own contribution is likely to affect her personal life, savings and time. Think about how her life will be different if she owns her own business rather than works for someone else.

Finally, suggest the benefits she would gain from running her own business.

Business	Type		
	Privately owned	State-owned	Voluntary or not-for-profit
HM Revenue and Customs			
Oxfam			
British Airways			
Barclays Bank			
Great Ormond Street Hospital for Children			
The DVLA			
The UK Passport Service			
Citizens Advice Bureau			
NSPCC			
Google			
Cancer Research UK			
your own school or college			

Activity 7

The *Sunday Times* 'Top Track 100' league table lists Britain's 100 biggest private companies. It ranks them by their sales, rather than by the number of employees they have.

Task 1

The table below shows some well-known companies listed with their 2006 rankings. Reorder it so that the businesses are ranked by number of employees, with the largest first.

Rank	Company	Activity	Sales (£m)	Staff
1	Gala Coral	Betting and gaming operator	7,433	17,189
3	Somerfield	Supermarket operator	4,589	53,011
16	Virgin Atlantic	Airline and tour operator	1,630	8,118
22	United Biscuits	Biscuit and snack maker	1,267	10,639
29	Sir Robert McAlpine	Construction contractor	1,092	2,278
35	BHS	Department stores	872	14,593
58	River Island	Fashion retailer	595	10,179
79	Southern Water	Water services provider	475	2,062
87	Harrods Holdings	Department store	448	4,099
90	Listers of Coventry	Car dealer	429	1,248

Sunday Times, 2 July 2006

Task 2

As a class, study your new list and suggest answers to the following questions:

- Which of the companies operate on a local, regional, national and international scale? If you are not sure, find out more about them online. You can easily find any of their websites by entering the name into a search engine.
- How can selling goods online affect the potential size and scale of a business?
- Gala Coral staff made sales worth over £400,000 each, whereas at River Island, the staff only managed to sell goods worth £58,000 each. What reasons can you suggest for this difference?
- Why would it probably be easier for you, as a student, to find out the number of staff in a private business than to find out the sales figures?

Activity 8

Divide into six groups. Each group should identify:

- a local business with fewer than ten employees, run by a sole trader
- a professional partnership in your area, such as a solicitors or accountants, with 10–20 employees
- a large business in your area (either a private or a public limited company) that operates on a national or international scale
- a medium-sized private company that operates only in your area
- the local authority for your own area
- the name of the local health authority and the largest hospital in your district

Compare your answers. Your tutor will then allocate one organisation to each group. Each group must then give a short presentation to the rest of the class, describing the business and stating its purpose, ownership, size and scale.

2   Classifying business activities

In this section we will focus on grading criteria P2 and M2 from Unit 1 'Exploring Business Purposes'.

You will look at the way business activities are classified into primary, secondary and tertiary sectors, as well as how these sectors are changing.

Learning outcome

Understand the classification of business activities

Content

Primary: e.g. farming, forestry, fishing, extraction/mining

Secondary: e.g. manufacturing, engineering, construction

Tertiary: e.g. private service industries, local and national public services, voluntary/not-for-profit services

Relative growth/decline by sector: decline of primary and secondary industries; growth of tertiary service industries

Grading criteria

P2: describe the primary, secondary and tertiary classifications of business activities using local and national examples

This means you need to know the difference between the categories, as well as which business activities belong in which category, and some local and national examples.

M2: explain areas of growth or decline in the primary, secondary and tertiary classifications of business activities

You need to know which sectors are growing and which are shrinking, and why. One approach is to identify where there are more job opportunities and where trades are dying out. Another is to look at profits being made: businesses will always be attracted towards profitable activities and away from unprofitable ones.

Activity 1

Task 1

Make a chart like the one below. Then enter each of the jobs listed in the correct column.

Primary	Secondary	Tertiary

- fisherman
- doctor
- army corporal
- writer
- airline pilot
- pig farmer
- plasterer
- aeronautical engineer
- coal miner
- printer
- actor
- teacher
- graphic designer
- bank clerk
- baker
- estate agent

Task 2

As a group, think of as many business activities and related occupations as you can that are connected, directly or indirectly, to the Glastonbury Festival – anything from fast-food caterers to tent makers.

Enter them in your chart under the correct categories.

Activity 2

Task 1

Working in small groups, identify four business activities carried out in your local area for each sector (primary, secondary and tertiary), and add these to your chart.

Primary	Secondary	Tertiary

Compare your ideas as a class. Enter all your ideas into your chart.

Task 2

On your own, choose four examples (two local and two national) from each sector on your chart.

Do *one* of the following:

- Write a brief description of each sector (primary, secondary and tertiary), using your selected business activities or occupations as your examples.
- Make a poster for display, describing each classification.

Task 3

Business activities grow or decline for many reasons. For example:

- fashions and trends
- lifestyles
- technological developments
- comparative prices (if products can be imported cheaply, they will probably no longer be made in Britain)

Working in small groups, identify as many products and services as you can, that you can buy easily now but that weren't fashionable – or didn't exist – 20 years ago. Ask your tutor for help if you get stuck.

Compare your ideas as a class.

Task 4

According to the Office for National Statistics, the primary and secondary sectors are declining relative to the tertiary sector, which is increasing.

Find out whether your investigations confirm this, by identifying the sectors to which the examples you and your group have just found belong.

Activity 3

Read the article below.

On the road to nowhere?

My grandmother sometimes talks of a time when Sheffield was famous for its cutlery, Lancashire for its textiles, Tyneside for its ships and the Midlands for its cars. She predicts the death of British industry. After all, employment in the UK car industry has dropped dramatically since the 1970s – and is still falling. In 2005, 10,000 people at MG Rover and its suppliers lost their jobs when the company collapsed and in 2004, 1,100 jobs were lost when Jaguar closed its factory. In 2006, Peugeot Citroën announced it was to close its plant at Ryton in Coventry and Vauxhall switched production at Ellesmere Port from three shifts to two with the loss of 900 jobs.

My grandfather takes a different view. He says 1.8 million cars were produced in the UK in 2005 – as many as during the peak years of the 1970s. They are made by Toyota, Nissan and Honda, as well as Ford, General Motors, Volkswagen (which owns the Bentley factory in Crewe) and the BMW Group – which owns Rolls Royce and the Mini factory at Cowley, Oxford. He argues that British manufacturing plants are now more efficient so there is less need for businesses to relocate to cut costs in the future. He also says that developed nations trade their skills and knowledge rather than basic products.

Grandmother isn't convinced. She reckons that it's risky when an industry is totally owned by foreigners, who may pull out at any time to save money. And even though UK manufacturing still accounts for two-thirds of UK exports and employs three million people, she is still convinced we will all work for retailers or in call centres before too long!

Task 1

Although far fewer people are employed by the car industry today than in the 1970s, the same number of cars are produced. This means that productivity has increased.

Suggest reasons for this increase.

Is this change good, or bad, for car manufacturers? Give a reason for your answer.

Task 2

As a class, discuss whether you think the UK car industry will one day disappear. Suggest reasons both for and against this view.

Task 3

Discuss the history of your own area with your tutor. Identify how the business activities and types of jobs in the area have changed over the last 50 years.

Task 4

Predict the future! What will jobs be like in 50 years' time? How likely is it that we will all work in shops or call centres by then?

Activity 4

News headlines often reflect sector changes, by reporting on the types of activities that are thriving and those that are not.

Here are some examples:

- Tesco's online sales have rocketed to nearly £1 billion and are continuing to grow at 25% a year.
- Shares in Southern Cross, Britain's largest care homes operator, have risen by 14% since it was floated on the Stock Exchange.
- Diageo, the world's biggest alcoholic drinks producer, announced an increase in sales of 6% for the year.
- Barclays announced it was restructuring and closing up to 200 branches and cutting about 1,200 jobs.
- Ryanair and Easyjet, the budget airlines, have both seen a sharp rise in passenger traffic, and Ryanair has bought ten more Boeing 737 aircraft for delivery in 2008.
- HMV, the books and music retailer, saw profits drop by more than £30 million in 2006.
- Floors 2 Go, the flooring retailer, reported that sales fell by nearly 9% at the start of 2006.
- British Sugar announced it was closing two of its UK sugar refineries at a cost of 219 jobs.
- Imerys is closing two china clay pits and one refinery in the West Country with the loss of 800 jobs. High energy prices mean UK operations are now uneconomic.
- DX Services, which provides business-to-business postal services, has been offered nearly £350 million for its business – more than 20 times its projected earnings for next year.
- George Wimpey, one of Britain's biggest housebuilders, announced it built more homes in the first half of 2006 than at any time for 25 years.
- Game Group, beloved by Xbox and PSP fans, announced higher sales throughout Europe, as well as in the UK and Ireland.
- According to the Society of British Aerospace Companies, 2005 was a bumper year for the British aviation industry. Jobs increased by 9%, and sales by 25%, with orders for new aircraft at an all-time high.
- Northgate Information Solutions, which provides software and IT support services, reported a 95% rise in profits this year.
- UK Coal announced the closure of the Harworth colliery, near Doncaster, which first produced coal in 1926.

Task 1

Working in small groups, for each of the news items above, identify:

- the sector in which that activity is classified
- whether the news item indicates a growth or a decline in that business activity
- whether you think the news is indicative of the overall trend for that sector as a whole (i.e., primary and secondary sectors declining relative to the tertiary sector, which is increasing)

Task 2

As a class, compare your answers, and then suggest reasons for the trends you have identified.

Activity 5

Task 1

Divide into three groups. Each group should focus on a different one of the three sectors (primary, secondary and tertiary), and investigate and summarise areas of growth and decline within it in the UK.

Task 2

Devise a poster to illustrate your findings. Use textbooks, the library and the internet to find the information you need. Include information you have already learned from the previous activities.

Present your poster to the rest of the class. See whether they can guess the key changes in the sector from the illustrations and clues you have included on the poster.

3   Business aims and objectives

In this section we will focus on grading criteria P3 and M1 from Unit 1 'Exploring Business Purposes'.

You will concentrate on business aims and objectives and how they vary between sectors. You will see how to compare and contrast organisations in terms of their ownership, aims and objectives.

Activity 2 also links to grading criteria P2 and M1 from Unit 3 'Investigating Financial Control'.

Learning objective

Understand business aims and objectives in different sectors

Content

Aims and objectives: aims (the long-term visions or goals of a business), objectives (specific, measurable targets to help achieve the overall aims of a business); purpose (to provide a business focus) eg survival, break even, growth, profit maximisation, service provision, expansion of market share; relationship with other businesses

Sector: e.g. private; public; not-for-profit and voluntary

Grading criteria

P3: describe the purpose of setting aims and objectives for businesses

This means you need to be able to say why businesses set aims and objectives and what they hope to achieve by doing so.

M1: compare and contrast the ownership, aims and objectives of two selected businesses

You need to choose two different businesses and say how their ownership and their aims and objectives differ. This is easier to do if you choose organisations that are totally different – for example, a large hospital and your local newsagent.

Activity 1

Remember: aims are long-term goals; objectives are shorter-term targets set to measure progress towards goals.

Task 1

Which of the items in the following list are aims and which are objectives? Using a table like the one below, put the items in the correct column.

Aims	Objectives

Put a tick beside all the objectives that are 'SMART' (specific, measurable, achievable, realistic, timed).

- Maximise profits.
- Grow the business.
- Offer home delivery in the local area.
- Reduce costs.
- Open two new stores next year.
- Increase sales by 5% by January.
- Expand market share.
- Survive.
- Break even.
- Increase number of subscribers by 10% within six months.
- Provide a service.
- Start a loyalty scheme.

Task 2

The Guide Dogs for the Blind Association has the goal of providing guide dogs, mobility and other rehabilitation services that meet the needs of blind and partially sighted people. It relies entirely on voluntary donations and legacies from the public.

a)   On your own, identify the type of ownership of this organisation.

b)   Working in a small group, suggest two aims it may have. For each one, choose and write down an appropriate objective. Then compare your ideas with other groups. If you need inspiration, access the website at www.guidedogs.org.uk.

c)   As a class, discuss how the aims and objectives of this organisation will be different from those of a large supermarket, such as Tesco. Then summarise your conclusions in your own words.

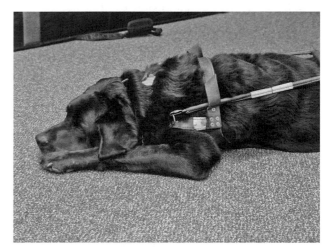

© Midiman, Flickr
(Public Commons)

Task 3

The Government has changed the rules governing how parking wardens can book motorists, after annual income from parking fees and penalties more than doubled to £1.2 billion between 1998 and 2006.

Local authorities can no longer set targets that encourage wardens to issue as many tickets as possible so that the authority can maximise income from parking fines. Instead, wardens must try to reduce the number of cancelled tickets and complaints from drivers about unfair penalties.

On your own, answer the following questions:

- In which sector are the Government and local authorities?

- What type of aims would you normally expect government departments or local authorities to have?

- Why was the Government unhappy about councils setting targets that encouraged parking wardens to issue as many tickets as possible?

© Gerry Davies

Task 4

Targets can sometimes have unintended consequences. What do you think happened when the following targets were set?

- New York police were set targets to increase their arrest rate.

- Hospital doctors were set targets to reduce the length of time people were in hospital.

As a class, compare your answers. Then discuss the sort of targets your tutor might be set that might have unforeseen consequences – and what these might be.

Activity 2

Chelsea FC, bought by Roman Abramovich for a cool £500 million in 2003, has announced its aim of breaking even by 2010. The club now boasts 4 million fans worldwide and matchday revenues of around £1.5 million. But income is only half of the story. A key objective is to reduce the amount spent on players' wages from 76% of turnover to 55%. The club has a way to go. Good players aren't cheap, and on total sales turnover of £146 million in 2005, the company made a loss of £140 million.

Task 1

On your own, try to answer the following questions:

- Identify one aim and one objective of the club.

- Stamford Bridge holds 42,000 people. Assuming it is regularly full, what is the average price of a ticket?

- If costs remain the same, how much must Chelsea earn each year to break even?

Task 2

Divide into small groups to see how well you would run a football club with financial problems.

Imagine your club has difficulties like those of Chelsea. Brainstorm the actions you could take to reduce costs and increase revenue. Then identify how each action would affect the break-even point, and make a shortlist of six things you would do immediately.

What would you do – and why – if you received the following news?

• Your two top players want to move to another club.

• The supporters' club is arguing that season tickets are too expensive because the team's performance is poor.

• For the last few weeks the pitch has been waterlogged so matches have been repeatedly postponed. A wet winter is forecast.

• Your main sponsor says he doesn't want to renew the contract at the end of the season.

Note down all your proposals and ideas on a flipchart page, then present them to the class. Your tutor will then decide which group would be the best at football club management.

Activity 3

Below are some objectives that have been announced by well-known organisations.

Working on your own:

• match up the objectives to the organisations listed

• suggest an associated aim for each organisation

• identify an aim that applies to all these organisations

Compare your answers as a class.

Objectives:

A. Open a new juice bar every six weeks.

B. Launch a movie download service.

C. Increase the number of stores it opens each year fivefold by 2008–9.

D. Launch 100 new products, including baked-bean-filled sandwiches that can be put in a toaster.

E. Link up with Ebay to sell adverts online.

F. Launch a new mobile phone service so that users can access the service wherever they are.

Organisations:

1. Heinz

2. Yahoo!

3. MySpace

4. Sainsburys

5. Channel 4

6. Crussh ('the natural fast food chain')

Activity 4

What went wrong?

The 2006 FA Cup final was supposed to be played, on Saturday 13 May, at the brand-new Wembley Stadium. Instead, it was played in Cardiff, after the target date for completion was put back to 2007.

Wembley's builder, Multiplex, has denied being at fault, blaming constant design changes by Wembley National Stadium Limited (WNSL), the FA subsidiary that is managing the project.

The key issue is who picks up the bill. When any project overruns, costs increase and it takes longer before any revenue is earned. A penalty clause in the contract for £140,000 a day will cost Multiplex a lot of money if it is enforced.

Working in small groups, try to answer the following questions. Then compare your ideas as a class.

• Why is it harder to meet aims and objectives on large projects?

• Why is a penalty clause often included in business contracts for major projects?

• Why might Multiplex want to blame WNSL for many of the delays?

© Martin, Flickr
(Public Commons)

4   Functional areas of business

In this section we will focus on grading criteria P4, M3 and D1 from Unit 1 'Exploring Business Purposes'.

Even in a small business, different employees do different jobs, each focusing on a key function of the business. Each of these functions is necessary for the business to run effectively. In a large business, people working on the same function usually work together in a department – for example, sales, marketing, customer services, or finance.

In these activities you will look at the main functional areas and departments, how they relate to each other, and how they can contribute to the aims and objectives of an organisation.

Activity 2 also links to Unit 6 'Providing Business and Administration Support', Activity 4 links to Unit 2 'Developing Customer Relations', Activity 8 links to Unit 3 'Investigating Financial Control', Activity 9 links to Unit 5 'People in Organisations', Activity 12 links to Unit 8 'Doing Business Online', Activity 13 links to Unit 7 'Personal Selling', and Activity 15 links to Unit 4 'Business Communication'.

Learning outcome

Know the main functional areas that support business organisations

Content

Functional areas: e.g. administration, customer service, distribution, finance, human resources, ICT, marketing, sales, production, research and development (R and D); purposes of functional areas e.g. to support business aims and objectives, to develop new markets, to support continuous professional development

Relationships: links and interactions with other functional areas

Grading criteria

P4: describe the functional areas and their main purposes within business organisations

This means you need to be able to say what the main activities are that are undertaken by different functional areas.

M3: explain the interaction of functional areas and how they relate to each other in two selected businesses

Here you will have to explain how functional areas communicate with each other and work together in two businesses you know well.

D1: evaluate how the functional areas contribute to the aims and objectives of the two selected businesses

This means you will need to look in detail at the targets or roles of different functional areas (departments) and identify how successful they are at helping the business to achieve its aims and objectives.

Note that M3 and D1 are covered in more detail in Section 5.

Activity 1

All organisations need administrators. These often work within different departments, rather than in a special 'administrative' department.

Task 1

As a class, brainstorm questions that you could ask one of the administrators in your school or college about his or her role.

Your questions should aim to find out about:

- the main activities undertaken by administrators
- typical communications and links with other departments or staff
- targets or objectives that link with the organisation's main aims and objectives

Task 2

In small groups, agree on between 12 and 16 good questions to ask, and put these together in a questionnaire that you could use during an interview with an administrator.

Present your questionnaire to the class, and then take a vote on which one is best.

Activity 2

Task 1

List the types of office equipment in your school or college office.

For each item, find out exactly what it does and how it contributes to meeting the requirements of the business.

Task 2

Find out more about the office equipment: in particular, how its facilities or features meet the requirements of the administrative staff. If the equipment does not meet the full requirements of the administrative staff, find out what additional facilities are needed and how these would help the administration of the organisation.

Investigate if there is enough money in the budget for the additional facilities.

Activity 3

Customer service can be provided face-to-face, over the telephone, or online. It can make the difference between a business with a good reputation and one which is often criticised or which receives negative publicity in the press and in TV 'watchdog' programmes.

Task 1

As a group, discuss the best and worst customer service experiences you have had – and whether these made any difference to your opinion of the organisation and your buying habits.

Task 2

Identify one type of business that regularly deals with customers (for example, a dentist, a shop, or a bank).

Then write a description of four different customers who may be difficult for the staff to deal with for some reason – for example, because of their special needs, expectations or attitude. Each one should be contacting the firm in a different type of situation (for example, visiting in person, telephoning, emailing, needing urgent attention, or making a routine visit).

Task 3

Exchange your scenario and list of customers with another group.

Read the list you have received and, as a group, suggest the best way of assisting each customer.

Identify the interpersonal and communication skills someone would need to be able to cope with each customer on the list effectively.

Assuming you ran that business, what presentation standards would you expect from your customer service staff?

As a team, present your answers to the rest of the class.

Activity 5

Queen of the road

If you thought everyone in the transport business was male, think again! In 1996 Hilary Devey set up her distribution business, Pall-Ex Ltd. On the first night, 29 hauliers handled 117 pallets of freight. In 2006 she was managing a multi-million-pound business with 280 staff distributing over 8,500 pallets a night. She also won the title of First Woman in the Business Services category of the First Women Awards run by the CBI and Real Business Magazine.

Her 'unique selling point' is a purpose-built hub with a network of members. Hauliers pay an annual fee to join. They can then bring deliveries on pallets from their own area and swap them for deliveries going back. This means they don't have to drive to multiple destinations, which increases efficiency and saves money.

Task 1

Find out more at www.pallex.co.uk.

Pall-Ex's hub is in Leicestershire. As a class, explain:

- why this location is suitable
- why the location of the hub is crucial to the success of the business

Task 2

On your own, identify the benefits for hauliers who join Pall-Ex. Then include these in a poster that Pall-Ex could put in transport cafes and other suitable locations to recruit new hauliers.

Task 3

Pall-Ex wants to promote its services in trade magazines. Working in pairs, investigate the website to find out more, and then draft an advertisement that describes Pall-Ex's main features as a distributor.

© Pall-Ex

Activity 6

Business owners usually consider finance the most important function. Unless the business earns enough money, and keeps a close check on its financial situation, it can get into serious trouble. No business can survive for long without making a profit.

In small groups, brainstorm all the different types of tasks that are carried out in a finance department or by someone who is responsible for finance.

You may be able to arrange to talk to someone from your college's finance department or to your school bursar.

Compare your ideas as a class.

Activity 7

Jason worked with two other part-time staff at a computer games store each Saturday. When they arrived last week they were all sacked. The manager had found some games stuffed into a waste bin near the back exit and suspected one of the Saturday staff was the culprit. Jason knew it wasn't him – but had no idea which of the other two was to blame.

As a class, decide whether Jason can do anything to keep his job or not.

If you work part-time, tell other members of your class about the precautions that your employer takes against theft and fraud, and the training you received to alert you to these issues. Then compare your experiences with those of other people in your class.

Activity 8

What went wrong?

Mobilride was a firm with a sales turnover of £2.5 million. One year later it had gone out of business because it could no longer pay its bills. What happened – and why?

Mobilride converted cars for use by disabled drivers. Its main customer was a large garage network that regularly supplied Mobilride with one make of cars, in batches, for conversion. This is labour-intensive work, so the wage bill at Mobilride was high – at about £700,000 a year. Mobilride also spent a lot on raw materials, and had borrowed heavily when it had cashflow problems in the past because it couldn't pay its bills. It borrowed to the maximum extent the bank would allow – so it had high loan repayments to make each month.

When Mobilride had cashflow problems again it cut its workforce to save money. But with fewer workers it took longer to convert cars. This resulted in delayed payments from the garage network, which only paid after completion and delivery of each batch. Then the car manufacturer switched production from the UK to Europe, which disrupted supplies. For three months, far fewer cars were received. Income fell alarmingly. Cashflow problems intensified. Mobilride delayed paying its own suppliers, who threatened to cut off all supplies. Mobilride couldn't operate without essential materials so had to pay some bills. Then one ex-worker, who had been sacked to save money, won his case for unfair dismissal and was awarded £40,000 by an employment tribunal. The firm couldn't afford the payment and had to close down.

Consider the following questions on your own:

- Identify the main source of cash inflows (revenue) for Mobilride.
- Identify three sources of cash outflows (expenditure) for Mobilride.
- What actions did Mobilride take to save money when it started to experience cashflow problems? How successful were these? Give a reason for your answer.
- What two events eventually caused Mobilride's demise?

To what extent could Mobilride's problems have been prevented by better cashflow forecasting or by better management? Discuss your ideas as a class.

Activity 9

The 'human resources' department is concerned with the people in the organisation at all stages of their employment – from recruitment until the day they leave.

Task 1

Work in small groups.

a)   Decide on the type of business you run, the job title, the salary, and the tasks you would want the person to do.

b)   Decide on a job vacancy at an appropriate level for your class. You can use advertisements in your local paper, or jobs advertised online, to give you ideas.

c)   Then prepare a job description, person specification and advertisement. The advert should tell people to apply by sending their CV and a covering letter.

d)   Circulate this around the class.

Task 2

From the jobs that are circulated, choose the one you would like to have. Then prepare your CV and a letter, targeting your application at that job, and send it to the group concerned.

Task 3

In your original groups, assess each application and decide its good and bad points and whether you would ask the sender to attend for interview. Justify your decision. Then give your feedback (sensitively) to each person.

Activity 10

The ICT department is responsible for the computer hardware, software and telecommunications in the organisation.

Find out more about the work carried out by ICT departments, by asking one of your college or school ICT staff to talk to your group.

Before the talk, make sure you are familiar with the ICT policy of your school or college. You can relate this to the type of security precautions in place to protect organisational data. As a class, agree on a list of ten questions that would be suitable to ask. Nominate someone to thank the speaker afterwards.

Activity 11

The marketing department is responsible for identifying customer needs and then promoting the business and its products or services in the most appropriate way. Marketing is concerned with attracting new customers, as well as communicating with existing customers.

Marketing professionals use a lot of jargon. On your own, see how many specialist terms and definitions you can link together from the lists below. Then compare your answers as a class.

Specialist terms:

A. direct marketing

B. tag line

C. sponsorship

D. endorsement

E. e-marketing

F. media

G. new media

H. reach

I. marketing mix

J. brand image

K. press release

L. PR (public relations)

M. promotional mix

N. viral marketing

O. podcast

P. search engine optimisation (SEO)

Q. campaign

R. microsite

Definitions:

1. traditional methods of mass communication, such as newspapers, magazines, TV and radio

2. promotion of a product or service, often by a celebrity implying that they use it or approve of it

3. giving financial or other support in return for recognition of a product or service

4. a linked combination of marketing activities

5. marketing using new media

6. a short article about a new development sent to the newspapers

7. digital and electronic methods of communication, such as the web and SMS messaging

8. when customers spread the marketing message themselves, for example by forwarding an email or text message to their friend

9. ensuring that the company website comes out as high as possible on search engines

10. free publicity about the business

11. sending information by post to customers who fit a certain profile

12. a slogan or phrase that summarises the theme of a campaign

13. the best combination of methods to achieve marketing goals and reach the target audience (for example, advertising, personal selling, online promotions)

14. the best combination of price, product, promotion and placement to maximise sales

15. the number of individuals who will receive the promotion message

16. a method of putting audio files on the internet

17. the way customers think of a brand and the associations they make

18. a miniature website created for a special purpose, often linked to a particular promotion

Activity 12

Online business is a combined effort between marketing, who decide the promotional aspects of the website, and ICT, who ensure that it functions well and is secure.

Work in small groups for this activity.

Identify three websites that you sometimes use between you. These should be as different as possible – in what they do (for example, sell goods, sell services or provide information), in their sector (for example, private business, government or voluntary organisation) and in the type of site (for example, very basic and passive, sophisticated or social).

Identify the main features of each website, and decide how the content has been designed to achieve the online aims of the business.

Present your ideas to the rest of the class.

Activity 13

The process of selling is vital to all businesses. You may be familiar with selling in a retail environment, but not with business-to-business sales. Often this requires deep technical know-how and experience, particularly for complex industrial products.

How good are you at selling? Find out by selecting two completely different products that you own (for example, your iPod and your course textbook), and deciding the best way to sell these to two different people (for example, one of your classmates and your tutor).

Tip: the best salespeople identify the benefits for the individual customer and sell those, rather than the features of the product.

Ask each person for feedback on your performance.

Activity 14

Everything you own or use has been produced somehow and somewhere – but the process will be very different for different types of product. You don't produce coffee in the same way that you produce paper, crisps, DVDs, or jeans.

However, all production processes have certain things in common: they all result in a product; they are all carried out in a logical order; they all take account of quality at different stages of the process. The best way to see how the production process works is to visit an organisation where something is produced – whether this is food, clothing, or any other type of product.

Divide into groups and find out how different products are made. Then report back on the process to the rest of your class. You can investigate products online, by researching in the library, or by contacting a local manufacturer. Example websites include:

- www.foodtech.org.uk (food)
- www.bigtimepictures.com/multimedia_process.aspx (DVDs)
- www.britishwool.org.uk/factsheet3.asp?pageid=96 (wool)
- www.greetingcardassociation.org.uk/info-resource/3d-cards/production-process-and-timescale (greeting cards)
- www.thetimes100.co.uk/case_study.php?cID=7&csID=30&pID=6 (chocolate)

A silent bike with a top speed of 50 mph, a range of 100 miles and zero emissions is every environmentalist's dream, although it might have to be adapted to broadcast an artificial engine noise to safeguard pedestrians. Another slight snag is that so far there is only one filling station in Britain (in Hornchurch). The bike uses fuel cell technology. Intelligent Energy, the company that developed it, still believes that the bike has a future – even with a price tag of around £4,500.

On your own, answer the following questions:

- Identify two major benefits of the bike.
- Identify two drawbacks.
- Do you think the bike has a future? Give a reason for your answer.

This is an example of R and D in the transport industry. Working in groups, suggest other examples in the following industries:

- aerospace
- pharmaceuticals
- IT or telecoms
- beauty
- food
- kitchen appliances
- one other industry of your choice

© Envbike

Activity 15

For a business to function effectively, all functional areas need to interact on a regular basis.

Task 1

Work in small groups to investigate the communications in your school or college.

With your tutor's help, identify one functional area for each group to investigate.

Find out the type of communications used by that functional area (for example, reports, emails, meetings, phone calls).

Identify two or three purposes of each type of communication.

Suggest what might happen if that functional area was not informed (or was misinformed) about an important development.

Put your findings into a table like the one below.

Task 2

Make your table into a poster and present it to the class.

Compare your findings.

Functional area:

Type of communication	Purpose	Consequences of poor communication

5   Obtaining and using information

In this section we will focus on grading criteria M1, M3 and D1 from Unit 1 'Exploring Business Purposes'.

You will learn:

- how to select a business to investigate

- the type of questions to ask to find out the information you need

- where you may have problems – and how to overcome these

- how to process your information to work towards achieving Merit or Distinction grades

We set out to find out about a local business. We describe what we did and you will follow us step-by-step. And then we will ask you to do something similar. This is not the only way to find out about business organisations but we hope it will give you some good ideas to use as starting points. And, remember, you will need to investigate *two* businesses.

Each activity takes you, step by step, through four stages.

The summary tells you what you need to do.

Any problems you may encounter, or important factors you should note, are given.

You see what we did when we investigated a business to find out the same information.

You try out the task for yourself. You can use one of your own selected businesses to do this, or if you are not yet ready to do that, as a group you may find it useful to investigate your own school or college.

Note: Our thanks are due to Liane Salthouse, Deputy Managing Director of Pavilion Communication Services Ltd, for her assistance with this section.

Grading criteria

M1: compare and contrast the ownership, aims and objectives of two selected businesses

This means finding out about these areas, and checking you understand them.

M3: explain the interaction of functional areas and how they relate to each other in two selected businesses

This means you need to understand what each functional area does and how different ones communicate with each other.

D1: evaluate how the functional areas contribute to the aims and objectives of the two selected businesses

This means you need to be able to link the aims and objectives to specific functional areas. There may be departmental targets – but this is not always the case. You also need to know whether the business has achieved all, or most, of its aims and objectives so far, and where there might have been any problems or weaknesses.

Activity 1

Select two suitable businesses to investigate.

Key points

Ideally, your businesses should:

- be large enough for functional areas of work to be identifiable
- be small enough that you can understand how the business operates
- carry out a business activity that you can understand without too much difficulty and that interests you
- be somewhere you know yourself (for example, because you work there part-time or have been there on work experience), or where you have a contact, such as a relative who works there, who can put you in touch with a senior person
- be near enough to visit (although it is possible to investigate a business by talking to someone on the phone, the website alone is unlikely to provide the information you need)

Alternatively, your tutor may recommend a suitable business, or arrange for local business leaders to talk to your group about their organisations.

Preferably your two businesses will have very different types of ownership (for example, public and private, or private and voluntary).

What we did

We listed all the businesses we knew about because we had friends or family who worked there or because we worked there (or had worked there) ourselves. We then crossed out those that were too large, too far away to visit, carried out very technical or complex activities, or were too small to have functional areas, or where the people we knew wouldn't be able to help us very much.

We then ranked those remaining according to the criteria above. The top business on our list was Pavilion Communication Services Ltd, an agency in Wilmslow, Cheshire, which produces creative campaigns for its clients using both traditional marketing and new media.

Your task

List all the businesses with whom you have (or have had) contacts. Write down the name, the address, the activity it carries out, and the contacts you have there.

Then check each business against the criteria above. Cross out any businesses that are very complex (so that you would struggle to understand how they operate) or very small, or where your only contact is at a very junior level.

Talk over your list with your tutor, and add any recommendations your tutor may be able to suggest. Then rank your businesses and decide which one to contact first.

Activity 2

The next step is to find out if someone senior in that business is prepared to help you. If you know someone who works there, ask for the name of the best person. Then ask your contact to talk to that person, explaining who you are and why you want to speak to them. An introduction like this makes it easier than approaching them directly. Make it quite clear that you want the information for a project you are doing for your BTEC First studies, and that you are not expected to obtain any confidential or commercially sensitive information.

Then telephone to make an appointment to speak to that person – but expect to have to work around their busy schedule.

Key points

Business people, especially in private organisations, are careful about information they consider to be commercially sensitive or confidential. This includes:

- financial information, if it is a privately owned business (public limited companies publish their accounts each year) – the owners or managers of a private firm will not usually want to talk about the value of their sales or how much profit they are making
- future plans (or changes to aims and objectives) that some of the staff don't yet know about
- problems or difficulties that the business owner wouldn't want anyone outside the company to know about
- any information the owner thinks could benefit a competitor

You don't need to obtain any confidential information (such as financial details). You will often have more success talking to someone in a private organisation if you reassure them on this point.

What we did

We found out that the best person to speak to was Liane Salthouse, the Deputy MD – but she was very busy. Our contact told us that she was happy to help, especially after we confirmed that we wouldn't be asking any questions that related to commercially sensitive or confidential information. We fixed a time and date to speak to her, and scheduled our day around meeting this commitment.

Your task

Find out who you should speak to and try to arrange an introduction to that person through your contact. Then agree on a time to meet that person – or speak to them over the telephone. Make sure this is one or two days ahead, so that you have time to prepare.

If necessary, reassure everyone that you are not expected to obtain any sensitive or confidential information.

Activity 3

It's now imperative that you do your homework about the business you are investigating. You can expect the person you contact to be busy, to speak quickly, and perhaps to use terms and jargon you don't understand. You will make life easier for yourself if you prepare in advance. This will also prove your own interest in the project and gain you more respect from the person you talk to. Also think about the questions you need to ask.

Key points

Don't expect to understand everything you read on the website, or expect this to have been written for students. It will have been designed to give information to the key customers. So if it is a shop, it will focus on products for sale; if it provides a business service, it will explain this in technical terms.

Focus on pages you do understand, and check out news items for current developments. Highlight any terms you don't understand and look these up.

Talk to your tutor if there are still some that you don't understand.

What we did

We accessed the website of Pavilion Communications and read every page. We also searched under Google for other relevant information and articles on the company. We looked up words and terms we didn't know. We made a note of the mission statement and checked out their news page, so that we knew what they had achieved recently. We printed out pages that were important.

We then looked back at the criteria for the assessment and wrote out a list of questions to prompt us, so that we didn't forget to ask something important.

Your task

Check out the website of the business you are investigating. Highlight any words you don't understand and discuss these with your tutor. Print out pages that relate to your investigations – for example, a mission statement, aims, objectives and functional areas. Do a web search for any other relevant pages (such as newspaper articles on the business).

Write out a list of questions you think you should ask, and check these with your tutor. Then compare it with our list (below). You may have thought of some good questions to ask that we didn't.

The questions we asked:

1. What is the full name of the organisation?

(If this ends in Ltd or plc then this tells you about its ownership. In this case you won't need to ask Q2.)

2. What is its ownership?

3. What is the main purpose or business activity of the organisation?

(Ask for specific examples of products or services if you are given a general explanation you don't understand.)

4. What is its size, i.e. the number of employees?

5. What is the scale of its operations (e.g. regional, national, European, global)?

6. What are the main aims or long-term goals of the organisation?

7. What objectives or targets have been set to help to achieve these aims?

(Public-sector organisations often set and publicise specific SMART departmental targets; so do large public limited companies. Smaller, private firms often do not.)

8. What are the names of the departments, or functional areas?

(These may vary from the standard names, depending upon the industry.)

9. What work is carried out by each of these departments or functional areas?

10. How do these areas liaise and communicate with each other? Please can you provide two or three examples in each case.

11. How successful has the business been in achieving specific aims and objectives to date?

12. Are there any functional areas that you plan to strengthen, so that you will be more successful in achieving your aims and objectives in the future?

Activity 4

Talk to your contact. If you are meeting them in person, make sure you are dressed appropriately. Be punctual. Arrive early for a meeting; and if you are making contact by phone, ring at the agreed time. Make sure you have a notepad and pen to hand so that you can make full notes on the responses to your questions.

Key points

If your contact would rather phone you, and you give your mobile number, fix an appropriate time to receive the call, so that you can plan to be somewhere quiet. Don't even think about trying to talk to someone in a businesslike way in the middle of the shopping centre or when you are with friends.

Be prepared for your contact to use some words and phrases you don't understand. Politely ask what these mean: don't pretend to understand something when you don't.

Bear in mind that functional areas may be called different things in different industries. If necessary, ask your contact to tell you what they do, and write this down.

Arrange a way of making contact again, in case you need to query anything you have written or

you think of additional questions you should have asked.

What we did

We talked to our busy contact on her way to a meeting. She was being driven, but spoke to us on her mobile during the trip. We took notes, and needed to clarify some specialist terms she used. We also agreed to email her with the notes we made, so that she was happy that we had noted down our facts correctly. This also gave us the opportunity to query any points we were uncertain about and ask one or two further questions.

Your task

Talk to your contact, obtain answers to your questions, and make notes. Don't forget to check words or phrases that you don't understand. Don't worry, either, about asking your contact to slow down if he or she is talking too quickly. Just ask nicely!

Concentrate on the conversation and what you are being told. This will help you to recall the information more easily afterwards.

Activity 5

The next step is to write up your notes. It's sensible to do this quickly, particularly if your handwriting isn't very good and much of what you've written was scribbled in haste. It is useful to include the meanings of any terms or explanations you were given, in case you forget them. Use a format that makes the information clear and easy to use.

Key points

Look up terms or words you've never heard before in a dictionary. You can also find out about most business terms in Google by typing 'define' followed by the term.

If you can't understand something you've written, leave a blank space and come back to that part afterwards. Then try to recall the conversation – or talk it over with your tutor. If you are totally stuck on one section, but everything else is clear, then you will have to ring your contact, apologise, and ask for clarification.

What we did

We wrote up our notes and put the information about functional areas into a table. Because some of these areas were different from the standard ones, we made a note of the type of work carried out by each one. We also noted the meanings of any special terms.

Our notes are shown below.

PAVILION COMMUNICATION SERVICES LTD – NOTES

Pavilion is an agency which devises creative campaigns using traditional marketing and new media.

Main purpose

Pavilion provides two main services for its clients:

- It improves their marketing performance, and this helps them grow their business.
- It improves their efficiency through technology. It installed an EPOS system for one client which improved its in-store communications. For another it built an extranet to improve communications between the client and two associate businesses.

Size

Pavilion is quite a small business. It employs 23 full-time staff.

Scale

National. It provides services for UK companies relating to UK work, but this is now changing and it will be undertaking international work for one client.

Ownership

Pavilion is a private limited company and was established in 1986.

Aims

To grow organically* and improve profitability. It aims to do this by enhancing awareness and reputation to attract new clients and raise its profile. This is because the better its reputation, the more high-calibre staff and blue-chip** clients it will attract, the better work it will do and therefore the higher the fees it can charge.

* This means to grow itself, without taking over or merging with any other businesses.

** Blue chip = a large organisation with a good reputation and which is financially stable.

Objectives

To achieve these aims its objectives include:

- to provide excellent client services
- to ensure its staff are highly skilled and motivated
- to win more awards
- to increase income from new media
- to keep debts owed to the business to a minimum

Functional areas

- creative
- technical development
- media
- client services
- operations (this includes HR, finance and admin)

Functional areas and relationships to objectives

Functional area	What it does	Relationship to objectives and responsibilities
Creative	Creatives are the 'ideas' people who design the campaign, for example devising the concept and content of the Star Wars interactive ads the company produced for a client.	They need to be top notch and have strong ideas and high-quality work to add real value to a client's business, to win clients at pitch* and to win awards. They are fundamental to the reputation of the business. * Pitch is the presentation of the proposed campaign to a client.
Technical development	They use technology to put the creative ideas into practice, such as doing the coding (i.e. programming) required, using Flash and other packages, to produce the Star Wars adverts (see www.pavilioncommunication. com/Showcase_June05/fight.htm – and turn the sound up on your speakers to get the full effect).	They must do high-quality work and be highly skilled to make the maximum use of the latest technology. They also produce technical solutions that Pavilion can sell on licence* to clients, which improves profits. * On licence means the client pays a licence fee to use the software.
Media	Media can be offline (e.g., press, TV, radio, posters) and online (e.g., websites, search engine marketing, banner ads and podcasts).	They are responsible for taking the clients' messages to the target audience. They buy media space and also track online campaigns to prove their effectiveness to clients.
Client services	Similar to 'customer services'. Staff are responsible for looking after clients and ensuring their needs are met.	They are key to the performance of the company. They are involved in meeting clients, costing projects, building relationships, pitching for new work, pulling projects together and ensuring the client's requirements are communicated to everyone in the company.
Operations	HR – High-calibre, motivated staff are vital to achieving the business's objectives. Pavilion operates a bonus scheme and sets objectives for staff linked to company goals. It also issues staff surveys to obtain the views of staff so that it can take these into account. HR works with the managers to support staff and achieve these aims. Finance – They pay bills, invoice clients, monitor cashflow, chase up payments when they are overdue to reduce debts owed to the company, and provide financial information for managers. Admin – They ensure the office operations run smoothly, and provide constant support for managers and staff, e.g. by arranging meetings, making travel arrangements, providing paperwork.	

Liaison between functional areas

- Client services produce briefing documents for each department that give details of customer projects.
- For each new project a 'kick-off' meeting is held to go over all the requirements.
- There is a management meeting every month, which involves the managers of all functional areas.
- Client services email everyone each week with 'where we are now/existing business updates'.
- Each team meets every Monday to discuss current and new developments and work in progress.

Current performance and effectiveness

The business is thriving and growing. It has won new clients and improved its client base. It now has a broader spread of clients, rather than just one or two who produce most of the revenue, which is always risky.

It has changed the way it is managed and has appointed departmental heads. It has also introduced a successful bonus scheme linked to a performance management project for staff.

It has expanded its new-media operations.

It has won awards, e.g. the Big Chip Award for the Best Digital Marketing Campaign and the Roses Advertising award in 2006.

Working with well-known brands has meant it has generated more PR, as these campaigns are covered by the trade press. This has a knock-on effect for new business.

Current improvement plans

Both these relate to client services.

1. Pavilion has recently been quite reactive to client needs and has built relationships with clients naturally rather than planning to improve or promote these. The account managers* will now be trained to develop client relationships more systematically. In addition, there will be an annual client survey used to track improvements.

2. Future business forecasting will be improved to track more precisely when they can expect to receive future business from current clients. This will improve the ability of the client services team to forward-plan their future income.

* Account managers look after the needs of one or more major business clients.

Your task

Write up your own notes, using the best format for recording your information and referring to it later. Check your finished work with your tutor. You should be able to explain what is written – and all the terms that you have used – without any difficulty.

Activity 6

The final stage is to link your information to the questions. This is important. You can't just reproduce your notes – you have to link them to the grading criteria in Unit 1 of the specification. This means you have to be able to:

- compare and contrast the ownership, aims and objectives of two businesses (M1)
- explain how the functional areas interact and relate to each other in both businesses (M3)
- evaluate how the functional areas contribute to the aims and objectives in both businesses (D1)

Remember, you will need to investigate *two* businesses. In our example above we have investigated one so far.

Key points

- 'Compare and contrast' means identifying the similarities and differences. Do this first of all by identifying the ownership of both businesses; then explain what each type of ownership means and how it links to the main purpose or aims. Then include the objectives, and say how these are different from the aims because they link to the aims of the business.
- 'Explain' means you must be able to say what each functional area does (i.e., the work it carries out), how it relates to other areas, and how these areas communicate. You should have this information in your notes.
- 'Evaluate' means you have to look at the current performance of the business, i.e., how well it has achieved its aims and objectives. Identify its strong points and any perceived weaknesses; then see how these provide evidence for the effectiveness of each functional area.

You will probably find it easier, and less confusing, to concentrate on one business at a time, when you are tackling the questions relating to functional areas.

What we did

We started by making notes to help us to write a full answer. This was particularly important for the evaluation, because we had to analyse our information to see what it told us.

The notes we made are shown below.

ANSWER NOTES

D1: Evaluation of Pavilion Communication Services Ltd

Assessment of each functional area:

- *Creative:* The business has won awards for its creative work, so this must be very good. Gaining awards will increase the profile because of publicity and articles in the trade press. Creative has also contributed to winning new business from well-known brands and gaining a broader spread of clients.

- *Technical development:* This area directly helps profitability by producing software solutions which are sold under licence. It also contributes to the achievement of the awards, e.g. the programming of the Star Wars campaigns.

- *Media:* This area directly contributes to the objective of increasing income from new media, and has expanded. Because its online campaigns can be tracked, these must have been successful for it to be winning new business.

- *Client services:* This function has to provide excellent services because these are essential to improve Pavilion's reputation and attract new business. It liaises with other areas through its briefing documents and weekly emails to keep them informed. It has been considered too reactive to client needs, and its forecasting also needs to be improved for it to contribute more effectively to the achievement of the aims and objectives.

Operations:

- *HR:* HR ensures staff are highly skilled and motivated, and monitors this through the staff survey. This is important to attract and retain talented people. It also monitors the achievement of staff objectives linked to the bonus scheme. Bonuses help to motivate staff.

- *Finance:* Good financial control, and ensuring debts are paid promptly, is essential to achieving profitability. Better forecasting by client services will help to improve cashflow forecasting, too. The fact that staff bonuses have been paid means the firm must be profitable.

- *Admin:* Good admin helps to free managers and creative/technical staff from day-to-day business worries, such as arranging meetings and travel and having the correct paperwork. Again, because the business is thriving and has an excellent reputation for its professionalism, this function must be effective.

Your task

Compare and contrast the ownership aims and objectives of the business you have investigated, either with your school or college or with Pavilion Communication Services Ltd. Then compare your ideas.

Write your own explanation of the way the functional areas interact and relate to each other in the business you have investigated. Alternatively you can use our notes to do this for Pavilion. Check your ideas with your tutor.

Evaluate how well the functional areas contributed to the aims and objectives of your selected business, using the evidence you have obtained. Make notes based on your information and look at each functional area separately. Again, check your ideas with your tutor.

Marked assignments

Exemplar assignment – Ref 2.3

Background information

Tesco is the most successful British supermarket, selling more goods and making higher profits than any of its rivals. It is also one of the world's leading international retailers.

Tesco says that its success is based on listening to people – both those who shop there and those who work there. Its core purpose is to create value for customers to earn their lifetime loyalty, and its core values are 'no-one tries harder for customers' and 'treat people how we like to be treated'. (Source: Tesco website.)

In this assignment you will carry out research on Tesco by reading newspapers and researching online to find out more about its customer service and how it monitors and evaluates this. You will also be asked to provide other examples from your own experience. These may be businesses you have visited as part of your course, a business where you work (or have worked) part-time or on work experience or one you frequently use as a customer yourself. You can also use information in your class handouts and relevant textbooks to help.

You will use your knowledge and research to identify customer service improvements and to explain and analyse the benefits that can be achieved to help the owner of a new small business.

This assignment will enable you to show that you can:

- (P3) Describe how consistent and reliable customer service contributes to customer satisfaction.

- (P4) Describe how customer service can be monitored and evaluated.

- (M3) Explain how monitoring and evaluating can improve customer service for the customer, the organisation and the employee.

- (D2) Analyse, using examples, how effective customer service benefits the customer, the organisation and the employee.

Remember that you must list your reference sources at the end of your work in a bibliography. This should include the titles of websites and newspapers or magazines you have used, the titles and authors of textbooks you have referred to and information on any other customer service booklets or documents you have quoted.

Task 1 (P3)

Alex is starting up her own retail clothes business and will employ four members of staff. She doesn't know much about customer service and doesn't seem to realise how important it is. She knows you are studying business and has asked for your advice.

Describe how consistent and reliable customer service contributes to customer satisfaction.

Write to Alex to help her understand the link between effective customer service and customer satisfaction.

a) List six factors and say how each one relates to customer satisfaction e.g. value for money – the rest of the examples should be from underpinning knowledge. Give examples for each one from your research of Tesco etc.

b) Using the template below, help Alex to achieve consistent and reliable customer service by identifying ten factors to be considered and how these can be actioned. Two factors have been given to get you started.

Achieving consistent and reliable customer service	
Factor to consider	**Action to take**
Scope of staff job roles	
Staff knowledge of products/services	

c) Alex's customers will also expect her to have ethical standards. Explain what this means and give two examples of selling goods 'ethically'.

Task 2 (P4)

a) Prepare a list of five methods used by businesses to monitor their customer service e.g. information customer feedback. For each item, explain what it means. Where you can, from your research and reading, give examples of well-known businesses that you know use these methods and the type of action they have taken as a result.

b) You can also advise Alex that she can use data about her own business to evaluate her business e.g. the level of sales. List five items of data and in each case:

i) state how Alex could obtain the information she needs

ii) describe the trend she would want to see to confirm that her customer service is effective

iii) from research and reading, suggest the type of action she could take to achieve this.

Task 3 (M3)

Explain how monitoring and evaluating can improve customer service for the customer, the organisation and the employee.

Alex wants to take some ideas about customer service to her next meeting with the Small Business Adviser at her bank. She has asked you to help her by writing a report for her. Prepare this document in which you will explain the improvements that could result if she monitors and evaluates her customer service.

a) Choose a suitable title for your report and state its purpose in your Introduction.

b) Then divide the report into three main sections, each with a clear heading:

- Improvements for the customer

- Improvements for the organisation

- Improvements for the employee

c) Complete your report with a Conclusion.

i) Use your research into Tesco to highlight the type of improvements the organisation could make as a result of its monitoring and evaluating.

ii) Suggest appropriate improvements that Alex may make. List the benefits she would obtain from 8 improvements that she should consider in order to maintain satisfied customers and good staff e.g. better quality of service.

Task 4 (D2)

Sometimes effective customer service and improvements can have an unexpected effect. When banks introduced cash machines they thought everyone would benefit. Customers could obtain cash 24 hours a day, the organisation could handle more customers with fewer staff, and the existing staff would have more variety in their jobs. However, there have been a few problems. There are often long queues at cash machines and sometimes the money can run out! There have been security problems in some areas with customers getting mugged when they leave a machine or finding their card has been cloned. Fewer staff in the branches has meant customers complain that there are longer queues when they do need to see a cashier, and fewer staff has also meant fewer job opportunities in banking. Banks have additionally been the targets of bad publicity when they have then increased their profits.

Even Tesco hasn't been immune to bad publicity. Because it is so successful, and its sales are always increasing, it is often seen as a threat to smaller shops and stores. It has been criticised by the media for being too big and too powerful and this has resulted in negative publicity for the organisation despite its good customer service record.

These examples show that even the best ideas and achievements may have limitations – and what is good for some people may have a negative effect on others.

Therefore to analyse how effective customer service benefits the customer, the organisation and the employer, collect the following research for a presentation to show examples of:

a) effective customer service at Tesco and one other contrasting business of your choice from the following list:

- your school or college

- another type of public sector business, such as a hospital or the police

- a business you use yourself, such as your bank, your doctor or dentist, your local bus company or cinema

- any other business of your choice, in agreement with your tutor.

b) For each of the examples you have found, identify the benefits to the customers, the organisation and the employees at each organisation.

c) Analyse these benefits by considering whether there may be any problems or limitations with each one. You will have to think about the people who may be affected, the cost of implementing the benefit and other relevant issues.

d) Produce a presentation to include the following steps:

i) give a definition of effective customer service

ii) list the benefits gained by the customer, organisation and employees for each customer service example for Tesco

iii) analyse each benefit to identify any limitations or other issues that Tesco should consider

iv) repeat iii) above for your chosen business

v) explain how the ability to analyse customer service benefits can help business people like Alex.

Pass level answers

Jack Evans – Assignment 2.3, Task I

> Alex is starting up her own retail clothes business and will employ four members of staff. She doesn't know much about customer service and doesn't seem to realise how important it is. She knows you are studying business and has asked for your advice.
>
> Describe how consistent and reliable customer service contributes to customer satisfaction.
>
> Write to Alex to help her understand the link between effective customer service and customer satisfaction.
>
> a) List six factors and say how each one relates to customer satisfaction e.g. value for money – the rest of the examples should be from underpinning knowledge. Give examples for each one from your research of Tesco etc.

- confidence in service;
- value for money;
- repeat custom;
- word-of-mouth reputation;
- internal customer/staff satisfaction;
- poor communication.

Customer satisfaction means customers are satisfied with the service because their needs are met. This means that they can find what they want and buy it at the right price and don't have to wait too long. It also means that staff are polite and helpful to them. This has to happen all the time, not just once or twice. If a customer isn't satisfied, even just once, they might decide to go somewhere else in future.

All these factors are all important for customers to be satisfied.

1. *Confidence in service*. Customers won't be confident if someone lies to them or doesn't know what they are talking about but pretends that they do. Staff should look up information before they pass it on and check it is right. The product must work and do what it says it will do and customer must know if they have a problem they can take it back and get help quickly. If a customer is let down by a business then this will destroy confidence.

2. *Value for money* means that customers don't feel ripped off. They may be able to check prices on the Net to see who is cheapest before they buy anything. Even people with lots of money who can afford expensive things still expect value for money. Tesco has a good idea with its price check promise so customers can check prices elsewhere. Customers can also buy value goods or Finest goods depending on how much they want to spend and this is good because it gives them a choice. Amazon sells value for money goods because you can buy the same things cheaper than in other places. People don't like iTunes because they don't think it is value for money when they have to pay 79p for every track but haven't any choice if they have an iPod.

3. *Repeat custom* means customers keep going back and they won't do this unless they are satisfied all the time. This means businesses don't have to work so hard trying to get new customers. Tesco started its Loyalty Card so that customers earn points and this helps to make sure they keep going back.

4. *Internal customer/staff satisfaction*. An internal customer is another member of staff you work with. If they want something then you have to provide it or they can't do their job properly. So in Tesco, if customer service call out for someone to help a customer, someone should answer. In our store, there was no-one to serve people at the fireworks stand for ages and they lost lots of customers trying to find him. This is not good customer service and the woman on the customer service desk wasn't satisfied with it at all.

5. *Poor communication*. This can happen if the customer doesn't understand the person speaking, such as at a take-away if they don't speak English very well and can't understand your order. It can happen if people are passing on messages and get it wrong so that a taxi doesn't go to the right address or the driver doesn't knock on the door and keeps people waiting for ages and then wants more money. This doesn't help customer satisfaction. If people answering the phone are rude then this annoys a customer too as well as if they are kept waiting for a long time. Staff should smile at a customer and get help if they don't understand something.

b) Using the template below, help Alex to achieve consistent and reliable customer service by identifying ten factors to be considered and how these can be actioned. Two factors have been given to get you started.

Achieving consistent and reliable customer service	
Factor to consider	**Action to take**
Scope of staff job roles	Make sure staff know what they can and cannot do as part of their job and the type of issues they must refer to a supervisor but make them use their initiative to resolve straightforward problems quickly. Don't let them overstep their authority. Staff must know what they are selling and where to find it so that they can tell the customer.
Staff knowledge of products/ services	Staff who know this can give advice on the best buys for a customer.
Type/quality of products stocked	
Attitude and behaviour of staff	Staff must be polite and smart and helpful all the time.
Timing	Staff mustn't creep up on a customer and startle them or harass a customer and if they phone at the wrong time they must ring back later.
Accessibility/availability of stock and staff	Customers get fed up if what they want is out of stock or if there is no-one around to serve them.
Meeting specific customer needs	This means finding out exactly what the customer wants and then selling it to them.

Achieving consistent and reliable customer service	
Factor to consider	**Action to take**
Working under pressure	Staff musn't get annoyed if they are busy or panic. If they get mad with the customer the customer won't come back again.
Confirming service meets needs and expectations	This means checking the customer is happy afterwards.
Dealing with problems	Staff often have to deal with problems such as customers who don't know what they want or things out of stock or selling something that doesn't work. Each member of staff should know what to do in this situation and get help if necessary.

c) Alex's customers will also expect her to have ethical standards. Explain what this means and give two examples of selling goods 'ethically'.

Selling ethically means not lying or doing anything that is illegal. It also means not doing anything to fool the customer like clocking a car so that the mileage is less than it really is or saying a car hasn't been in a crash when it has.

Assessor Feedback Form

Learner Name: Jack Evans

Assignment Ref 2.3, Task 1 (P3)

Jack, you have made a useful start on this assignment but it needs some more work doing on it to achieve a pass standard. Nothing you have said is wrong and you clearly understand the subject. However, more information needs to be added to several sections. Also, try to avoid using slang expressions such as 'ripped off', 'fed up' and 'get mad'.

a) In your explanation of the meaning of customer service you should also include other types of situations, such as where a service is provided and when an online purchase is made. It would also be good to think of an alternative word to 'satisfied' in the first sentence.

In your section on confidence, you are going rather too far by suggesting that staff lie. It would be better to focus on what staff can do to make sure their information is accurate.

Your section on 'value for money' reads well but the next one on 'repeat custom' needs expanding. You could say more about loyalty cards and also suggest other ways in which businesses encourage customers to return – for example by sending discount vouchers through the post.

You have missed out the 'word of mouth' section completely so you need to put this in. In the next one on 'customer/staff satisfaction', you need to give more general examples and also say how staff satisfaction contributes to customer satisfaction.

The section on poor communication could also include examples of both written and verbal communication problems. Remember what you have discovered from your research into Tesco – such as the 'customer service champions' who greet customers.

b) Your description of each factor is correct but each section needs expanding. There is no link to your own experiences or your research on Tesco or your class handouts. Alex needs as much information as you can provide.

c) You have given two examples of unethical practice but you were asked to give two examples of ethical selling, so you will have to redo this section. Remember that there is a difference between ethical practice and complying with the law! Look back at your class handouts and your textbook if you have forgotten about this.

Remember that there is no need to copy out the question – save yourself some time! Also, the task you were set was to write a note to Alex so you should begin your answer with 'Dear Alex' and finish it appropriately. ALWAYS read the instructions for a task carefully. Finally, you should not copy word for word from text books as you have done for the first item in section b. Use your own words to show that you understand the topic.

Read this feedback carefully and then do the work required to achieve a pass. I suggest that you do this before starting task 2.

Nazeem Patel – Task 1

Dear Alex

You wanted to know about customer satisfaction. Customers are satisfied when they can get what they need. Their expectations are also important. So customers visiting your shop will be satisfied if they find clothes they like which are a good fit and good value for money. Everyone expects to be served by a polite person who is helpful and knows the stock. Customers prefer to try on clothes in private and expect the shop to be clean. Many businesses want customers to be delighted, not just satisfied. For this to happen they have to get better service than they expected. This is why Tesco has its 'Every Little Helps' programme because it wants to keep improving the shopping trip for its customers so they are constantly delighted with the experience with 'clear aisles, no queues, great staff, good prices and what they want is always available'.

All the following factors relate to customer satisfaction as you will see.

1. *Confidence in service.* Customers must be able to trust you and your staff and know what you say is true. They must trust that the clothes are well-made and won't fall apart and that if that happened you would help them. Otherwise they would tell their friends and this would lose you business. You must also keep your promises to people otherwise they will think you are unreliable and go somewhere else.

2. *Value for money.* This does not mean things must be cheap. Tesco says that customers say that they like the Finest range, which is really the most expensive, because it 'represents great quality and value.' People think Tesco clothes are good value for money too. As an example their school uniforms are cheaper than many other shops which saves families money and it is good not to spend very much on children's clothes when they are growing fast. Topshop also sells good value for money clothes which is why it is so successful and you will need your customers to think that yours are too.

3. *Repeat custom* means your customers keep coming back and this saves you money because you don't have to spend as much advertising for new ones as your happy customers will tell their friends to come. There are lots of things businesses do to try to get customers to keep coming back. Tesco has its loyalty scheme where customers get points when they shop and it also gives them vouchers to get extra points and save money on petrol and things like that. This wouldn't work with a

clothes shop like yours, though. But getting people to collect things can work, like the coupons Tesco gives for computers for schools. Johnsons the dry cleaners has a priority club for regular customers and they get cheaper cleaning. Some dress shops have a club and members get alterations free or invites to sale previews so perhaps you could do something like this.

4. *Word of mouth reputation.* This is what people say to each other about your business. They will tell their friends if they like your business and this will bring you more new customers, whereas if they criticise you to their friends then this will lose you business.

5. *Internal customers/staff satisfaction.* Your staff won't give customers good service if they are unhappy. They need to get on with each other and to help each other to do a good job. They should not be stressed or upset. Tesco says it wants all its staff to 'enjoy their work, be healthy, safe, well-rewarded, trusted and respected'. It also trains them so that they know what they have to do properly. They know that everyone is important for the store to work, not just people who talk to the customers. Your staff will have to know this too.

6. *Good communication* helps customers to be satisfied. This means they are told something that is true and they can depend upon it. Your staff must be able to listen carefully and ask tactful questions and be polite. They must not shout and if they try to pressure people into buying then this can put many people off. They must not use body language which says they are impatient or annoyed. They must use words people understand and not use slang. If your staff are bad communicators this will annoy and lose customers, so they may need to be trained to do this properly. If you send letters to customers these must be polite and your adverts must be clear so that customers understand them. Tesco has Customer Champions in many stores who are specially trained. They welcome people to the store, answer questions and give help and have been specially trained to help people. Some other businesses have special Greeters at busy times. Perhaps you could do the same thing.

You also need to think about consistency and reliability. This means that you give the same standard of customer service all the time and everyone does this. To help you I have included this table.

Achieving consistent and reliable customer service	
Factor to consider	**Action to take**
Scope of staff job roles	Staff must know what they can and can't do as part of their job role. Tesco issue clear job descriptions and make sure every member of staff knows what sort of problems they can solve themselves and those that they must refer to a supervisor.
Staff knowledge of products/ services	Your staff must know the stock and where it is found. You will need to tell them when new stock arrives – perhaps they can help to unpack it. They need to know about prices of different clothes so that they can recommend them to customers. They also need to know if you do an alteration service and what it costs and how long it takes. Many businesses have staff training days once a week early in the morning so that they are up-to-date on new stock.
Type/quality of products stocked	This means that your staff will be able to recommend the best purchase for each customer and won't say something isn't available when it is. They should also offer to get something for a customer if it is out of stock.

Achieving consistent and reliable customer service	
Factor to consider	**Action to take**
Attitude and behaviour of staff	Staff must not chat together in a group because this annoys customers who think they are being ignored. They need to be well dressed and smart and be pleased to see customers and want to help them. Some businesses give sales staff commission to encourage them to make sales although Tesco doesn't do this but Richer Sounds, the hi-fi and electrical shops does. It has quite a complicated reward scheme but basically this rewards staff who customers say are very helpful.
Timing	It is really annoying if customers have to wait for ages on the phone before anyone answers or if they are in a long queue on a phone or at a counter. Tesco has its 'one in front' policy so that queues are very small. Your staff should also say hello to people when they enter the shop and then wait and let them look around for a bit before they go to them.

Achieving consistent and reliable customer service	
Factor to consider	**Action to take**
Accessibility/availability of stock and staff	If you want your customers to be satisfied then you will need to have a good range of stock in all the most popular sizes. It is even better if you can get clothes quickly if people want to order something in a different size but they shouldn't have to buy it unless they know it fits. It is also important that you have enough staff so that customers aren't kept waiting too long even when you are very busy. This is why many shops have Saturday staff or part-time staff who only work on busy days.
Meeting specific customer needs	Your staff will need to be able to talk to customers to find out exactly what they want. Some customers have special needs. They may have a young child with them, they may be disabled or blind or deaf. They may be in a rush at lunchtime and have to go back to work. Tesco identifies special customer needs by talking to its customers and then doing things like making sure people in a wheelchair can move around easily. It also has baby changing rooms and special parking spaces and has clear signs for people who cannot see very well. You could find out more about helping disabled customers and do that in your shop.

Achieving consistent and reliable customer service	
Factor to consider	**Action to take**
Working under pressure	People are more stressed if they have a boss who is really critical so you should help your staff if they are very busy, not just tell them what to do. They must know what you want them to do first, which should be to help the customer and not to do something less important like tidy up.
Confirming service meets needs and expectations	You should check the customer is pleased with the service you have given. If they are a regular customer then you can ask them next time they come in. If you have their telephone number then you can make a quick phone call to check they are happy with everything. Or you could write to them and ask them to fill in a form but many people can't be bothered to send it back. Customer happy calls are made by many firms including Richer Sounds and many garages when someone has bought a new car. You could perhaps just do this for customers who have spent a lot of money or bought clothes for a special occasion.

Achieving consistent and reliable customer service	
Factor to consider	**Action to take**
Dealing with problems	Your staff must know what to do when there is a problem such as if someone returns something because it is faulty or because they have changed their mind. You must offer to give them their money back if it is faulty but you don't have to do this if they have just changed their mind. It might help if you list all the problems they might have and what they must do and train them properly. This will mean everyone will always do the same thing and if the problem is very serious they will refer to you. All the large stores, including Tesco, have complaints procedures which all the staff must follow.

You also need to understand about selling clothes ethically. This is not the same as obeying the law about selling. It means things like being honest about what the clothes are made of and where they were made because most people wouldn't want to buy clothes made by child workers who were paid slave wages even if they were very cheap. Many large firms like Tesco say that they trade ethically. For example, they won't buy from suppliers who use child labour or have dangerous workplaces or treat their workers cruelly. You can read about it more at www.ethicaltrade.org. You are different because you only have a small business but it is still important that people know that you are truthful and will help them if they have a problem and do the best that you can and this means that you are ethical.

I hope I have helped you.

Good luck!

Nazeem

Nazeem Patel – Task 2 (P4)

a) Methods of monitoring customer service

1. *Informal customer feedback.* This means talking to customers to see what they think about the business and its products or services. For example, in a restaurant, the waiter should check the customer is happy with their meal and the service. Customers can also often make comments to people like receptionists, retail assistants and customer services. On a train people may say something to the conductor who checks their ticket if they are fed up because they have had to queue for ages or can't sit down because there aren't any seats. This information should be passed on because it helps the business to find out what people think.

Tesco has a Freephone customer service helpline people can ring and holds Customer Question Time sessions in its stores to find out what people think. This means they can find out what the customers think about their products, prices and other services. Tesco says this is how it has learned how customer attitudes are changing and that they now want more healthy, organic and local products.

Harley Davidson, the motorcycle manufacturers expects its managers to spend up to 15 days a year taking a ride with customers to find out what they think informally.

2. *Customer questionnaires/comment cards.* Many businesses use these. Questionnaires are designed to find out customer views on certain things. They can be given to people, sent by post, done over the phone or online. Hotels and airlines and travel firms often give them to customers at the end of their holiday. Debenhams has an online customer panel and Tesco also does them. Our college issues questionnaires to students twice every year to find out what they think about their courses and college facilities like the library. Richer Sounds gives out till questionnaires to customers who can win a prize for completing it and sending it in.

Comment cards are different to questionnaires. Tesco customer comment cards are available in all their stores so people can fill them in before they forget if they are bothered about something. Richer Sounds has 'We're Listening' cards in its stores that people can complete to give feedback. Some restaurants put comments cards on the tables for customers to complete when they have finished their meal.

At our college the opening times of the refectory were changed because of comments students made in their questionnaires. Tesco has also used feedback from local customers to decide what sort of products to stock in the stores they use, such as more Polish products in UK stores now there are more Polish people living in England.

3. *Staff feedback*. This means obtaining information from staff. They need to be able to pass on comments customers made as well as saying what they think, too. They should say if they have problems and if they think of good improvements to their jobs. Tesco hold Staff Question Time sessions and have Staff Forums too. They also asks for anonymous feedback in their Annual Viewpoint survey and have a Pulse survey too, which asks staff what they think about working for Tesco.

Richer Sounds holds Listening Sessions with its staff and two ideas it adopted were installing bells in the doorways for disabled customers and redesigning the catalogues to make them better. It also has an annual Colleague Attitude Survey which staff complete anonymously. This tells managers the things staff like and don't like.

4. *Mystery Customers*. Mystery shoppers aren't real customers. They are employed by agencies to visit a business just as if they are a real customer to see what type of experience real customers have. The business then gets a report on what happened. Richer Sounds uses them and so do other firms.

5. *Complaints and compliment letters* are received by all businesses. People who complain expect a reply. As well as replying to these letters the business should collect them and look at the reason they were written. If there are lots of complaints about the same thing or the same person then something needs to be done about it. Letters can be logged under different types of complaint, such as whether it was about prices or service or staff. This tells the managers if there are problem areas in the business that need to be sorted out. Compliments should be passed on to staff as everyone likes to get a compliment and it helps to encourage staff to work harder. In some places, such as hospital wards, cards saying 'thank you' are pinned up on a noticeboard so everyone can read them. In others, such as hotels, they count towards making an employee the 'employee of the month' and may help them to earn a bonus.

b) Evaluating customer service

Alex can evaluate customer service by obtaining information to help her to know whether her customer service is good or not. The information she needs is:

1. The level of sales

Alex can add up her till receipts every week to see how many things she has sold and how much money she has taken. It is better if she knows exactly which products she has sold because then she knows which ones are popular and which ones are not. Most cash registers do this and on the receipt it says the item and the amount. If customer service is good then every week her sales should increase and this is the trend she would want to see.

Tesco has a very sophisticated computerised system which prints detailed receipts. Tesco analyses sales to see what individual customers are buying and this helps them to decide what to stock in different stores. They also tempt customers to spend more by giving them vouchers to increase sales.

2. Number of repeat customers

Alex's customers will come back more if her customer service is good so she wants to see this trend. Alex needs to know which customers are repeat customers. She could start some sort of Loyalty Card herself to help her to check which customers are coming back rather than just try to remember them. She could give these customers something special like free alterations or early warnings about her sales and invite them to special events too.

3. Number of new customers

Alex also needs new customers and could tempt them with offers like printing a coupon in the paper which is worth money and gives the customer a discount. Lots of businesses do this like hairdressers, camera shops and, again, Richer Sounds. Many businesses give rewards to customers who recommend a friend so perhaps she could do this too. If she was always getting more new customers she knows she is doing well.

4. Level of complaints/compliments.

Alex won't want lots of complaints. If she has had a lot she will want the trend to show these are going down. She will like compliments and will want these to increase as these show that her customer service is good.

5. Staff turnover.

This means the number of staff who are leaving to work somewhere else. This happens if staff are unhappy. Alex then has to find new staff and they have to learn about the business, so it is better to keep good staff. Sometimes, though, people may leave who are happy but have no choice, like someone who is moving away. She will want her staff turnover to be low and to stay that way.

Staff are more likely to stay if they are paid fair wage and given interesting jobs. Tesco says it does this and aims to keep over 80% of its experienced staff by giving them training and benefits eg flexible working hours and childcare vouchers.

Assessor Feedback Form

Learner Name: Nazeem Patel (2)

Assignment Ref 2.3

Task 1 (P3)

Nazeem, this is a very good assignment and has achieved P3 – well done! You show that you understand the subject very well.

There are a few minor areas where improvements could have been made. Read them and bear them in mind as general guidelines when you are working on future assignments or towards a Merit.

First, in section five on internal customers/staff satisfaction, you could have also pointed out the value of team work which makes work more enjoyable for staff and this would reflect in their attitude to their customers.

Under 'type/quality of product stocked' you could have also looked at a situation where it is not possible to obtain the item a customer wants, which could be the case at the end of the season in a clothes shop. In this case a good assistant would discuss alternatives.

When you deal with how businesses should cater for customers with specific needs you may find it easier to write about customers with disabilities separately from those with other special needs – such as customers in a hurry or with young children.

Remember, too, that when you are talking about staff working under pressure, the key point is that they can prioritise, so that they tackle the important and urgent jobs first.

Finally, when you talk about ethical business, you could also mention selling goods at a reasonable amount based on their cost price.

Overall you have worked very hard on this section and researched it well. There are some very good examples and you have made all the points relevant to Alex's business and given her some good ideas about customer satisfaction. You have included several quotes from your research on Tesco, which is good. Remember that you will need a bibliography at the end of your work to say where you found your information.

Task 2 (P4)

Nazeem, overall this is a very good assignment and clearly achieves a pass standard (P4). Below I have listed a few small points where minor improvements could have been made. I hope you will find these suggestions useful when you continue to work towards a Merit grade.

a) In the section on Customer questionnaires you could also have mentioned the information we did on YouGov surveys in class and it is always worth mentioning that it is better to allow staff in an organisation to complete questionnaires on their work anonymously, otherwise they may hesitate to write anything critical.

Two points to note on complaints and compliments. Customers often expect *action* on a complaint, not just a reply. If the problem cost them money and/or caused considerable inconvenience they may expect money as compensation. However, it is not always possible to solve every complaint. Remember that when we studied Richer Sounds and their customer service, we found that they divide complaints into two categories – those which can be solved and those which cannot. An example of the former would be a customer being given wrong information and one of the latter, poor parking facilities in the locality.

b) When you talk about the level of sales you should advise Alex that these can fluctuate on a short term basis – some weeks will be better than others. She must keep an eye on longer term trends. A similar argument applies to the next section. Alex would like to see the number of repeat customers increasing over time.

You should stress that, ideally Alex should not receive any complaints but if she does, they must be acted on quickly and thoroughly.

I very much enjoyed reading this assignment. You have carried out a lot of research and describe things clearly. Don't forget to add a bibliography – remember I mentioned this last time.

You are now in strong position to work on M3, which I know you want to achieve so that you can progress smoothly to BTEC National level next year.

Good luck.

Merit level answers

Faizal Ahmed – Assignment 2.3, Task 3

REPORT FOR ALEX

Improvements for the customer

If you monitor and evaluate your customer service then your customers will gain many benefits and will notice an improvement almost straight away. This is because you will make changes they want. You will find out what they want by giving out questionnaires or comment cards and when you read these you can make the necessary changes. Tesco has a 'one in front' policy at its tills because it found that customers don't like to queue. You could do this, too. Tesco sells successfully online and you may want to try this too so that customers don't have to bother visiting the shop. Tesco also opens 24 hours in some stores because customers like to shop flexibly, so you might want to think about this too. If you make the changes people want then you are more likely to attract new customers and increase your sales.

Improvements for the organisation

Your business will see improvements because more customers and more sales means you will make more profit. More customers will come back, too, which is also good, because they will know they can rely on you.

Improvements for the staff

Tesco listens to its staff by issuing questionnaires and it also does surveys. It lets staff fill them in without putting their name so they will tell the truth. It also has a staff magazine called One Team and has Staff Question Time meetings. You won't be able to have a magazine because you only have a small business but you could have staff team meetings. It is better if you do this outside the business and perhaps take them out for a pizza to talk about what they think.

If you listen to what your staff say and do this then this will improve the conditions for your employees and therefore you will keep your staff. This will save you employing and training new people. If you are making a lot of profit then you can also give them bonuses which will help them to stay with you. You also need to find out about things like health and safety and all the laws about employing staff.

Assessor Feedback Form

Learner Name: Faizal Ahmed

Assignment Ref 2.3 Task 3 (M3)

Faizal, I am sorry to say that this is a poor effort – not up to your usual standard. I will discuss it with you at your personal tutorial next Wednesday. In the meantime I want you to think about the issues listed below so that when we meet you will have some ideas about how to improve it.

There are two main overall problems. The first is concerned with the structure of the assignment. You were asked to submit it in report format – remember we prepared an example in class a few weeks ago. Go back to your notes and refresh your memory. The main points are that reports should be produced in numbered sections with headings – including an introduction at the start and conclusions at the end – which was also mentioned in the assignment brief.

The second main problem is that, while you have not said anything which is wrong, you have not supplied enough information and explanation in any of the three sections. I have given more details about this below.

Under 'improvements for customer' the points you give in relation to Tesco are fine but you have not really translated them into Alex's situation – a small shop. For example, whilst avoiding queuing is a universal problem, small businesses may not have enough money to set themselves up to trade on the internet. Many are simply happy to use it to advertise. Also, small businesses cannot open 24/7 but it may be useful for them to consider adjusting opening hours to meet customers' needs.

Your section on improvements for the organisation needs quite a lot of work. You need to give much more explanation. For example you must identify relevant improvements Tesco has gained as an organisation such as increasing sales, market share and profit and then apply these to Alex's business.

The section on improvements for staff starts well. For example you have adapted ideas from Tesco to suit Alex's situation. You should have taken this further by taking more Tesco-based initiatives such as wage levels and the actions they take to retain experienced staff.

Faizal, I'm sure that you can improve on this. Remember that at Merit level you have to provide evidence that you have researched the topic well and you must answer the question fully. I know that you want to progress to BTEC National next year, and these skills will be doubly important then!

Emily Cox – Assignment 2.3, Task 3

REPORT ON IMPROVEMENTS TO BE GAINED FROM MONITORING AND EVALUATING CUSTOMER SERVICE

Introduction

This report explains the improvements that can be gained from monitoring and evaluating customer service. As examples it uses improvements and benefits Tesco has gained and looks at which ones could be appropriate for a small clothing business.

Improvements for the customer

Tesco has introduced several improvements after monitoring and evaluating customer service and listening to its customers. These have included:

- Matching the stock in a store to suit the customers who shop there
- Keeping the prices low and comparing prices online with its competitors
- Improving the checkout service to reduce queuing
- Aiming to give all customers a great shopping experience
- Training staff to make sure they know the products and how to talk to customers and help them
- Making sure the selling areas are kept clean and tidy
- Giving customers a choice of payment methods
- Employing Customer Champions to greet customers as they enter the store and answer any questions
- Having a comments box in the stores for customer suggestions
- Enabling customers to buy online as well as in a store
- Having Clubs like a Food Club and a Baby and Toddler Club and sending out information such as recipes to customers who join these clubs
- Making shopping as easy as possible for customers with disabilities.

You could use some of these ideas. If you monitor and evaluate your customer service then customers will gain because:

- You can make sure you stock the clothes they want to buy and change your stock if it isn't selling.

- You can check your prices aren't too high and so stop people coming to your shop.

- Your customers will enjoy shopping at your shop and it will be more fun.

- Your service will be better because staff will be well trained, will know how to greet and deal with customers properly, they will know what is in stock and be friendly and helpful.

- You can keep a list of regular customers and send them information and perhaps special offers through the post

- You could perhaps start a website and sell small items this way, like belts and scarves or just use it to advertise the business and put the website name on your carrier bags

- You can check that disabled customers can enter and leave the shop easily and know how to help them

- You will not be breaking any important laws, like those on health and safety.

- If you take notice of customer comments then your customers will feel important and know that you care about them.

Improvements for the organisation

As an organisation, Tesco is very successful. Everyone has heard of Tesco and most people have shopped in a Tesco store at one time or another. They keep making record profits. In 2005/6 their profit was £2.25 billion. They are also successful in other countries in the world, like China. They are also successfully selling non-food items like electrical goods and clothes. Tesco is also involved in charity work and has a Charity of the Year and is involved in the community in various ways, such as with its Computers for Schools vouchers.

If Alex monitors and evaluates her customer service then her business will gain because:

- More new customers will visit and more customers will return again and again.
- Satisfied customers will tell people so you won't have to spend as much on advertising.
- There will be fewer complaints which will save you time.
- The business will have a good reputation. This is especially true if you also do something for charity, such as hold a fashion show.
- Your sales and profits will increase.
- You could sell new products such as accessories or shoes and expand the business.
- You could open another shop and be successful because you have a good reputation.

Improvements for the staff

At Tesco these have included:

- All managers having to help and respect their staff
- Jobs designed to be interesting.
- Staff being encouraged to get on by taking qualifications or doing training.
- A benefits package and flexible working hours, childcare vouchers and a pension scheme.
- Trying to remove stress from jobs.

Monitoring and evaluating in your business could bring improvements for your staff such as:

- Your staff will know you care about them and want to help them so they will be more likely to work hard.

- Staff will be less likely to leave if they enjoy their jobs and can get on.

- The staff will enjoy their work more because they will know exactly what they have to do and how to do it.

- They will be able to rely on each other for help.

- If your business does well then you could give them a pay rise and perhaps a bonus as well.

- If your business does well then their jobs will be more secure.

- Your staff will know they are working in a healthy and safe place.

Conclusions

My conclusions are as follows:

1. Tesco is a good example because it listens to its customers and to its staff and has made many improvements as a result. It is very successful so this proves that monitoring and evaluating works. It says that 'listening to people and responding to what they tell us is vital to our success'. It also says 'We try to deliver what customers want and we treat people – customers and our team – as we like to be treated.' This is good advice.

2. Even though Tesco is a very big business there are still useful things to learn by looking at what they have done and this will help a small business like yours to keep improving and to be very successful too.

Emily Cox

6 November 2006

Assessor Feedback Form

Learner Name: Emily Cox

Assignment Ref 2.3 Task 3 (M3)

Well done Emily, this is an excellent piece of work – well up to M3 standard.

You have researched information from Tesco thoroughly and translated this into appropriate advice for Alex. There is nothing I would suggest to improve the content at this level. Apart from a couple of a couple of points (see below), the report is well structured with an Introduction, Conclusions and sections with headings as required.

In relation to the structure/style of the report, in the 'improvements for the customer section' you could have perhaps considered using sub headings for the two sections – the one relating to Tesco and the other to Alex's business. Often, if you have long sections in a report it is useful to break them up with sub-headings so that they are easy to read. In the section on improvements to the organisation, you could have used bullet points could have been used in the first part (Tesco) for consistency with the other sections.

Apart from those minor points, however, this is a very good report indeed.

You can now concentrate on working towards D2. Remember that to improve your work to Distinction level you will need to identify specific examples of customer service and analyse these to think about the benefits and drawbacks or limitations. For example, a benefit for Alex's customers might be to open longer hours on a busy day like Friday but this may not be very popular with her staff.

Finally, do remember you need to include a bibliography at the end of your assignment to list the sources of information you have used.

Distinction level answers

Ben Sharpe – Assignment 2.3, Task 4

Slide 1

Effective customer service

By Ben Sharpe

Slide 2

Tesco and effective customer service

Examples are
- No queuing
- Low prices
- Lots of choice
- Customer/staff feedback
- Customer service desks and customer champions to greet/help customers
- Interesting jobs and training

Slide 3

The effect of Tesco benefits

Customers:
Like no queues, low prices and lots of choice so give positive feedback. They can also see customer service staff if they have a question to ask.

The organisation:
Gets more customers because it gives value for money and good service so its sales and profits keep going up.

Staff:
Have steady jobs with good pay and are listened to. They also have good prospects and interesting jobs.

Slide 4

Problems and Tesco customer service

- No queues means it's a nuisance for staff if they have to stop what they are doing and go on a check-out.
- Low prices means they have to buy things very cheaply so some goods may be rubbish
- Giving people choice gives staff problems remembering everything.
- Lots of staff may not want to be bothered being trained and just want to do an easy job.

Slide 5

Customer service and our college

Examples are:
- Student Services to help people
- New car park just for students
- Resource Centre open in evenings and weekend
- ID cards for students
- New computers and laptops to borrow
- Stationery shop for students

Slide 6

The effect of college benefits

We can get to use computers more easily and finish our assignments at night if we want.	Not as many people are complaining about computers and parking.

Tutors don't have to talk about courses and grants because staff in Student Services do this for them.

Slide 7

Problems and college services

- There still aren't enough computers and we shouldn't have to pay for print-outs.
- Parking only matters for students with cars.
- Student Services is often too busy to help people and you have to keep waiting or come back later.
- Stationery shop is dearer than town shops.

Slide 8

Analysing benefits

This helps Alex not to think of benefits that most people won't like. She will also talk to her staff and customers to see what they think and this is important.

Assessor Feedback Form

Learner name: Ben Sharpe

Assignment Ref 2.3 Task 4 (D2)

Ben, I like some aspects of this assignment. Your slides are well designed and laid out. Also, you have effectively researched both examples of customer service – Tesco and your college.

Unfortunately, there are some areas which you need to improve to achieve Distinction standard. I will explain these below.

The task set asks for an introductory section defining effective customer service – you need to add this. You also need to amend the title of your presentation to show that you are *analysing* effective customer service, not just talking about it.

Slide three correctly has three headings showing the different effects of the benefits of customer service on the three groups – customers, the organisation and staff. You need to add these headings also to slide six – the effects of college benefits. Also you have summarised the benefits under each heading, rather than thinking about how each group could benefit from each of your examples. This has meant that you have missed out some of the effects of the benefits you have identified. For example, at Tesco, the organisation benefits from its policy of no queues because this improves the reputation of the business. Staff benefit because fewer customers will complain to them or be irritated when they reach the checkouts.

Using this technique, I'm sure that you can think of several additional benefits to add to the different groups at Tesco and the college.

The problems you have identified on slides four and seven are apt to focus mainly on one group of people. For Tesco, most of them relate to the staff, for the college they relate to the students. Instead you need to think of the negative impact of a benefit on each group. Therefore, for example, having a policy of no queues may also mean that Tesco has to employ more staff for busy periods which increases costs for the business. Also there are limits to how many checkouts can be provided in each store.

To improve your work to gain a Distinction you need to provide analysis. This means looking carefully at the good and bad aspects of a situation – in this case for each group involved. You also need to include a bibliography which gives your research sources for the whole assignment.

You have made a good start and I look forward to seeing your revised presentation. Do remember that when you give this you do need to look at your audience and not just read from your slides or notes. It is often helpful to practise beforehand. You should also be prepared to answer one or two questions at the end. You can use this as an opportunity to demonstrate that you understand the topic and have thought about the issues involved.

I am sure with a little effort you can soon improve this work and gain your Distinction grade.

Emily Cox – Assignment 2.3, Task 4

Slide 1

ANALYSING EFFECTIVE CUSTOMER SERVICE

Emily Cox

Slide 2

Effective customer service

- ☐ This is service that impresses customers because it gives them what they want
- ☐ It is also consistent and reliable so that customers can depend upon it
- ☐ 'Customers' can be external or internal (staff)

Slide 3

Examples of effective customer service at Tesco

- ☐ Can buy online and have goods delivered
- ☐ Low prices
- ☐ Can use self-service checkouts in some stores
- ☐ Loyalty card helps Tesco to understand what customers want
- ☐ Tesco Express stores are small shops specially for local neighbourhoods

Slide 4

Benefits of Tesco effective customer services

	To customers	To organisation	To staff
Buying online	Good if busy or housebound or not near a store	Increases sales and profits	Provides work for van drivers
Low prices	Saves money	Attracts customers	Staff customers will save money
Self-service checkout	Quicker	More sales	Makes life easier
Loyalty card	Gain points and benefits	Encourages customer loyalty	Staff can have one too
Local shops	Good for elderly	Increases sales	Can work near home

Slide 5

Limitations of Tesco customer services

Service	Limitations
Online shopping	Some customers don't have computers, staff doing orders can get in people's way in the store, delivery vans add to traffic, staff may pack the wrong things and annoy customers.
Low prices	Many people may think cheap food is no good or cruel, like battery hens.
Self-service checkouts	Customers may make mistakes or try to get things without scanning them. Tesco may cut staff.
Loyalty card	Some customers don't like Tesco knowing all about them and what they buy.
Local Express shops	May put other little shops out of business because they cannot sell things as cheaply as Tesco so they have to close.

Slide 6

Another example of effective customer service

At my doctor's
- ☐ New bigger premises with better facilities
- ☐ New women doctors in the practice
- ☐ Good appointment system
- ☐ Check-in-yourself system
- ☐ Electronic message board
- ☐ Can order prescriptions over the phone and have them delivered

Slide 7

Benefits of doctor's services

Benefit	For patients	For practice	For staff
New premises/ better facilities	Good reception and parking	Can offer more services	More space for everyone
Women doctors	Some prefer it	More services	New ideas
Appointment system	Saves waiting	Fewer complaints	Doctors' time isn't wasted
Check-in-yourself system	No waiting	Receptionist can do other things	Saves staff time
Electronic message board	Good to read when waiting	Gives new information to patients	Saves staff having to tell patients
Prescriptions	Saves time	Quicker	Easier

Slide 8

Limitations of doctor's services

Benefit	Limitation
New premises/ better facilities	Location not as good for many patients and some staff because is in different area.
Women doctors	Are part-time so hard to get an appointment.
Appointment system	Some patients may not turn up but doctors have to sit and wait for them.
Check-in-yourself system	Old people get confused and it might break down.
Electronic message board	Blind people cannot see it. Messages have to be clear and polite or can upset patients
Prescription service	Only available at certain times which annoys patients.

Slide 9

The benefits of analysing customer service

Analysing customer service will help Alex because:

☐ She can see which services have more benefits than limitations

☐ She can see who is affected by her improvements

☐ She won't introduce a benefit that would upset people.

☐ She will think about the things that might annoy customers or staff and perhaps change her ideas because of these.

BIBLIOGRAPHY FOR ASSIGNMENT 2.3

Tesco website: Annual Review 2006

Tesco website: Tesco corporate Responsibility Review 2006

Tesco website: www.tesco.com/customerservices/

Tesco.com – Competition Commission documents: Talking Tesco

Tesco website: www.tescocorporate.com

BBC news website: www.newsvote.bbc.co.uk:

BTEC First Business 2nd edition – Carol Carysforth and Mike Neild

Shearwater Surgery: Patient Handbook

Assessor Feedback Form

Learner Name: Emily Cox

Assignment Ref 2.3 Task 4 (D2)

Emily, you have produced a well-researched, carefully structured and presented assignment throughout and your presentation easily meets Distinction standard. You have made a big effort to identify the appropriate benefits of customer service aspects to each group and have obviously thought carefully about these. Even more importantly, you have analysed the various aspects well by identifying relevant limitations. Your bibliography is also good and you have used your evidence well. The witness statement I have also added shows that you gave careful thought to all the issues involved and explained these carefully at your presentation to achieve D2. Well done!

Just one minor point to bear in mind for your future business assessments. In the area of limitations you could have mentioned financial issues once or twice. Remember that all businesses, even doctors, have to keep an eye on the financial implications of all their actions and decisions.

Keep up the good work!

Witness Statement for Emily Cox

Presentation on Analysing Effective Customer Service

Analysing, using examples, how effective customer service benefits the customer, the organisation and the employee

Emily, you gave a very good presentation about analysing effective customer service by explaining what effective customer service means, giving several good examples both for Tesco and your own doctor's practice and pointing out the benefits to customers (or patients), the organisation and the staff in both cases. In addition you also highlighted some relevant limitations for both types of business.

Overall your approach was thorough and balanced, and you clearly showed that you understand that most things have a mixture of good and negative effects. You covered all the requirements of the assignment very well.

Your presentation style was good. You used your notes only occasionally and kept good eye contact with your audience. In addition you answered the questions at the end clearly and competently.

Well done!